A few years ago Arthur Deikman took part, as a professional psychiatrist, in a research seminar at the University of California at Berkeley on new religious movements, where former members of cults came to speak and interact with participants. Deikman was struck not only by how normal the people seemed, but also by how similar their experiences in cults seemed to all sorts of experiences we all share every day—in corporations, politics, psychiatry, and traditional religions. Most people regard cults as dangerous but rare; Deikman argues that the patterns of cult behavior are much more widespread than people think. Exposing these cult patterns in everyday life is the startling and original focus of *The Wrong Way Home*.

Deikman argues that the desires that bring people to cults—including the desire to feel secure and protected—are universal human longings. Their effect in our daily lives can be shockingly like the effect they have within the most bizarre cults, leading people to take self-destructive paths toward the security they seek: they can lead us to fail to think realistically, to suppress healthy dissent, to squelch our own autonomy, to devalue outsiders, and to accept authoritarianism.

The book begins with an extreme example: a nightmarish case study of a couple who became involved in a cult that ended up nearly destroying their lives. With this vivid case as a model, Deikman uses countless examples to show how many of our everyday relationships and institutions follow the same dangerous patterns. He talks about corporations' use of indoctrination, hierarchies, work schedules, and geographic relocation in forcing cult-like devotion and obedience. He writes about how the dynamics within political groups force suppression of dissent and scorn for outsiders. He exposes the ways in which traditional religions, which people don't think of as cults, show the cult-like tendencies of idolizing leaders and preventing independent thought.

THE WRONG
WAY HOME

Also by Arthur J. Deikman, M.D.

Personal Freedom

The Observing Self:
Mysticism and Psychotherapy

THE WRONG WAY HOME

UNCOVERING THE PATTERNS OF CULT BEHAVIOR IN AMERICAN SOCIETY

Arthur J. Deikman, M.D.

BEACON PRESS
Boston

Beacon Press
25 Beacon Street
Boston, Massachusetts 02108

Beacon Press books
are published under the auspices of
the Unitarian Universalist Association of Congregations.

97 96 95 94 93 92 91 90   8 7 6 5 4 3 2 1

Text design by Hunter Graphics

Library of Congress Cataloging-in-Publication Data
Deikman, Arthur.
    The wrong way home : uncovering the patterns of cult behavior in
American society / Arthur J. Deikman.
        p. cm.
    Includes bibliographical references and index.
    ISBN 0-8070-2914-9
    1. Cults—United States—Controversial literature.   2. Cults—
Psychology.   3. United States—Social conditions—1980–
4. Dependency (Psychology)   5. United States—Moral conditions.
6. United States—Religion—1960–   I. Title.
BL2525.D55   1990
302.3—dc20   90-52584
                                                                      CIP

To Henry and Gertrude Mandelbaum

Contents

Acknowledgments

This book was undertaken because of what I learned at a year-long seminar on new religions organized by Richard Anthony, Ph.D., Jacob Needleman, Ph.D., and Paul Schwartz, Ph.D., of the Center for the Study of New Religious Movements. I am grateful for the rich experience and creative environment they provided.

I am indebted to the many people whose work has provided substance for this book, especially Ben Bagdikian, Irving Janis and Idries Shah.

Useful comments and suggestions were made by a number of persons who read the manuscript or portions of it at various stages of its development: Walt Anderson, Ph.D.; Enoch Calaway, M.D.; Arthur Colman, M.D.; Etta Deikman; Charles Gompertz, D.D.; Lynn Howard; George Leonard; John Levy; Mel Morgan; Stuart Miller; Robert Ornstein, Ph.D.; Alan Skolnikoff, M.D.; Francis Vaughn, Ph.D.; Roger Walsh, M.D.; Margaret-Rose Welch; Leighton Whitaker, Ph.D.

Suzanne Lipsett, Joanne Wyckoff, Chris Kochansky, and Wendy Strothman gave valuable criticisms and editorial suggestions for which I am very appreciative. I would also like to thank Fred Hill for providing encouragement and help in bringing this work to publication.

Finally, I wish to thank "Hugh" and "Clara" for their courage in telling their story so that others would benefit.

Introduction

Much of my work as a psychiatrist consists of helping people become aware of the fantasies that influence what they do and how they feel. Interestingly, it is not fantasies of power and riches that cause the most trouble, but those of receiving protection, nurture, comfort, or praise; of someone keeping count, noting deeds, thoughts and efforts. It doesn't matter who a person is, no matter how outwardly independent, a child's wish for a powerful protective parent waits in the depths of the psyche and seeks expression. And express itself it does. The result is cult behavior even in people who do not belong to cults.

Usually, the word *cult* refers to a group led by a charismatic leader who has spiritual, therapeutic, or messianic pretensions, and indoctrinates the members with his or her idiosyncratic beliefs. Typically, members are dependent on the group for their emotional and financial needs and have broken off ties with those outside. The more complete the dependency and the more rigid the barriers separating members from non-believers, the more danger the cult will exploit and harm its members.

A number of books have been written about cults. Robert Lifton's landmark study of Chinese brainwashing, *Thought Reform and the Psychology of Totalism*, enabled us to understand the cognitive mechanisms operating in totalistic environments, where the authorities have complete control over people's lives and use any means to convert their subjects to their own rigid system of belief.[1] Lifton's analysis is very applicable to extreme cults, one of which I will describe in Chapter Two. But our everyday society is not totalistic. We are not subject to the total control possible to the Chinese communists (who held their prisoners by force), or to the psychologically coercive environments of the worst cults. Nevertheless, I will argue that behavior qualitatively similar to that which takes place in extreme cults takes place in all of us, despite our living in an open society, uncoerced, free to select our sources of information and our companions. We need to understand the cult behavior that operates unnoticed in everyday life.

Toward the end of his book, Lifton remarked that childhood helplessness and dependency produce "a capacity for totalism." I will focus in detail on the way in which the longing for parents persists into adulthood and results in cult behavior that pervades normal society. When I speak of a wish for parents I am not speaking of transference—the re-experiencing of a specific parental relationship—but of a yearning for parents in the most general sense. This longing results in fantasies of wise, powerful guardians even in those who are themselves looked up to by others, the best educated, the most cynical. Such fantasies exist in the borderlands of consciousness and may seldom be noticed, but they may be superimposed on people who occupy real positions of authority, success, and power, or their images may be displaced to a heavenly realm. Only by recognizing the indwelling wish can we gain freedom from the childhood world of vertical relationships and gain an eye-level perspective.

Such recognition is not easy. Freud made us aware that childhood experience may be expressed in the malfunctioning of the adult; this developmental understanding is now part of our worldview. But despite our sophistication in matters of individual pathology, we lack sufficient recognition of the dependency wishes that all of us express in covert form.

It is difficult to write convincingly about everyday cult behavior because some of the words I must use may sound like psychiatric jargon: dependency, unconscious fantasies, longings for security. Everyone exempts themselves from the description. The psychologically sophisticated are likely to think they are beyond these things and others may think that only weaklings have such vulnerabilities. To try to circumvent this problem I will make extensive use of examples drawn from a number of sectors of society: government, large corporations, the media, psychiatry, and religion.

The price of cult behavior is diminished realism. We cannot afford that now, if we ever could. Fortunately, awareness is a potent antidote. Increasing that awareness is the goal of this book.

The Cult Mirror

A FEW years ago I took part in a research seminar on new religious movements, the religious and utopian groups which sprang up in the sixties and seventies and made the term *cult* familiar to all newspaper readers.[1] Like everyone else, we in the seminar were impressed by the power of cult groups to dominate their members. A most extreme example was the People's Temple of San Francisco, whose mass suicide in Guyana was regarded as a piece of insanity, a horror that could be condemned without hesitation, in part because it appeared so alien to our lives. Other groups were only slightly less notorious for such activities as mass sterilization of their men or prostitution of their women; some cults engaged in the breaking up of families and financially exploited devotees, actions less newsworthy but nonetheless damaging.

In reading about cults, most of us in the seminar felt repulsion and fear, but also fascination. Cults present us with images of surrender, violence, sex, and power. We respond to them with avid interest because they speak to unconscious wishes. Moreover, we can watch at a seemingly safe distance because the cults of which we are aware usually have foreign trappings or unusual social structures that separate them from ordinary society and from ourselves. Without such markings, however, cult behavior is not usually recognized, especially when this behavior is our own.

Former cult members were interviewed by the seminar research group. We talked first with a man and a woman who had escaped from the People's Temple camp in Guyana on the morning of the mass suicide. These witnesses were not college graduates, nor were most members of the People's Temple. At subsequent meetings we interviewed a married couple who had belonged to quite a different cult, one whose members were highly educated, possessing graduate degrees in psychology or related fields. (They had worked as psychotherapists and teachers, just as we in the seminar did.) After that, people spoke who had been members of a utopian rehabilitation group for ex-convicts and, still later, we heard from members and ex-members of several other new religions.

The variety of personalities involved, of differing racial, economic, religious, educational, and social backgrounds, was impressive. What was most striking was that no matter whom we interviewed, the stories of involvement in exploitive, harmful cults were similar. A distinct pattern of seduction, coercion, corruption and regression emerged, no matter what the outward trappings, no matter what dogma or purpose the group espoused. Basic human responses had been elicited by a process fundamentally the same.

THE CULT STORY

At the time they joined their particular cult, most of the people we interviewed had been dissatisfied, distressed, or at a transition point in their lives. Typically, they desired a more spiritual life, a community in which to live cooperatively; they wanted to become enlightened, to find meaning in serving others, or simply to belong. An encounter with an enthusiastic, attractive, friendly person served to introduce each of them to a group whose outer appearance was quite benign. At some point during that introductory phase an intense experience took place which was interpreted as validating the claim that the leader and the group were special, powerful, spiritual; that they could give the person what he or she wanted. This experience might have been an altered state of consciousness (induced by the leader or the group via meditation, chanting, or the laying on of hands), a powerful therapeutic experience, or just a wonderful feeling of being accepted and welcomed—of "coming home."

Won over, the newcomer joined the group, embracing its doctrines and practices. Soon the cult's demands increased and the new member was asked to devote increasing amounts of time, money, and energy to the group's activities. These demands were justified as necessary to fulfill the group's goals; willingness to comply was always interpreted as a measure of the recruit's commitment and sincerity. In order to continue, most did comply, sacrificing much for the sake of the stated high purposes of the group (often put in terms of saving the world).

Relationships outside the group became difficult to maintain. The former life of the new member was given up; contact with outsiders was discouraged and the demands of the new life left little opportunity for extra-group activities. However, the sacrifices were compensated for by the convert's sense of belonging and purpose. The group and the leader (at least initially) gave praise and acceptance.

Gradually, however, an iron fist was felt. Deviation from group dogma brought swift disapproval or outright rejection. The message to the convert became clear: what the group had given the group could take away. In time, he or she submitted to—and participated in—cruel, dishonest, and contradictory practices out of fear of the leader and the group, who by then had become the convert's sole source of self-esteem, comfort, and even financial support. Actions that conflicted with the convert's conscience were rationalized by various formulas provided by the leader. (For example, in one group lying to potential converts was explained as "divine deception" for the good of those deceived.) Critical evaluation of the leader and the group became almost impossible, not only because it was punished severely, but also because the view of reality presented by the cult had no challengers. Discordant information was excluded from the group's world.

Exploitation intensified and the recruit regressed into a fearful submission. Couples might be separated; members would inform on each other. Morals were corrupted and critical thinking suppressed. Often the group's leader deteriorated as well, becoming increasingly grandiose, paranoid, or bizarre. In most cases, paranoid thinking tended to mark the entire cult and reinforced the group's isolation.

Our witnesses told of how, eventually, the demands became unbearable; a mother might be told to give up her child or her husband, or a spouse directed to take a different sexual partner. Although often the person would agree to the new requirement, sometimes he or she would not. In such cases, when the member finally refused to comply with the leader or the group's demands, he or she left precipitously, often assisted by a person outside with whom, some contact and trust had been maintained.

Leaving such a group was a flight because the group's reaction was known to be severe and punitive. Apostates were excommunicated. It was not uncommon for ex-converts to fear that they had been damned or had lost their souls as a consequence of leaving the group. (In some cases former members were convinced the group would hunt them down and kill them.) Many went through months of struggle to re-establish their lives, wrestling with the questions How could I have been involved in such a thing? How could I have done what I did to other members of the group? Were my spiritual longings all false? Who and what can I trust? At the same time, the closeness the group offered was often sorely missed, and until the ex-member's life was reconstituted, he or she wondered at times if leaving the group had been a mistake. This turmoil gradually diminished, but for many a sense of shame for having participated in the cult and a frustrated rage at having been betrayed lingered for a long time.

.　.　.

After listening to many variants of this story, I began to see that cults form and thrive not because people are crazy, but because they have two kinds of wishes. They want a meaningful life, to serve God or humanity; and they want to be taken care of, to feel protected and secure, to find a home. The first motives may be laudable and constructive, but the latter exert a corrupting effect, enabling cult leaders to elicit behavior directly opposite to the idealistic vision with which members entered the group.

Usually, in psychiatry and psychology, the wish to be taken care of (to find a home, a parent) is called *dependency* and this is a rather damning label when applied to adults. Adults are not supposed to be dependent in that way, relying on another as a child would rely on a mother or father. We are supposed to be autonomous, self-sustaining, with the capacity to go it alone. We do recognize that adults need each other for emotional support, for giving and receiving affection, for validation; that is acceptable and sanctioned. But underlying such mature *inter*dependency is the longing of the child, a yearning that is never completely outgrown. This covert dependency—the wish to have parents and the parallel wish to be loved, admired, and sheltered by one's group—continues throughout life in everyone. These wishes generate a hidden fantasy or dream that can transform a leader into a strong, wise, protective parent and a group into a close, accepting family. Within that dream we feel secure.

Who does not recognize the feelings portrayed in the cartoon on page 8?

The wish to ride in the back seat of the car—the dependency dream—has great strength and tenacity. It should be recognized as a permanent part of the human psyche even though in adults it ceases to be as visible as it is in childhood. This dream is dangerous because in its most extreme form it generates cults and makes people vulnerable to exploitation, regression, and even violence. Even in the less intense, less obvious manifestations which occur in everyday society, the dependency dream may impair our ability to think realistically. If we recognize our dependent wishes for what they are we can make appropriate corrections in thought and behavior, but usually we do not. Rather, we engage in thinking and behavior more subtle than that of the People's Temple but qualitatively similar. The back seat of the car does not carry us home.

Eventually, we in the seminar were unable to maintain the belief that cults were something apart from normal society. The people telling us stories of violence, cruelty, and perversion of values were like ourselves. After listening and questioning we realized that we were not different from nor superior to the ex-cult members, that we were vulnerable to the same dependency wishes, capable of the same betrayals and cruelty in circumstances in which our sense of reality was manipulated.

As I studied the psychological mechanisms that made the cult experience possible, I began to recognize uncomfortably familiar processes. A little reflection provided many specific instances of my own compliance—conscious and unconscious—with the values and preferences of my peers, compliance that I had rationalized or ignored because I preferred to think of myself as very in-

dependent. Since no radical change or disruption of my life occurred and I was not acting at the behest of a charismatic leader or occult group, it had not occurred to me that I might be behaving like one who has been captured by a cult. Nevertheless, I now realize that the motivations and manipulations constituting cult behavior are present in varying degrees in my own life and that they play a role in the lives of most of us as they operate in our educational systems, the business world, religion, politics, and international relations. Just as many of the more notorious cults have proven to be costly and destructive, so ordinary cult behavior is damaging and harmful to some degree wherever it occurs, no matter how normal its outward appearance.

When the seminar began I viewed cults as pathological entities alien to my everyday life. By the time it ended, I realized that the dynamics of cult behavior and thinking are so pervasive in normal society that almost all of us might be seen as members of invisible cults. In fact, as I will argue, society can be viewed as an association of informal cults to which everyone belongs. Yet the groups most of us belong to do not appear strange, flamboyant, esoteric, or unnatural, nor do they defy society with lurid and violent behavior. Social infrastructures and behaviors that are similar to those of the People's Temple go unnoticed.

Surely, the reader may ask, while it is true that serious consequences result from membership in extreme cults, how can you say harm comes from the groups that make up normal society? I certainly don't recognize such effects in groups to which I belong. I am indeed talking about normal society, in which the damage resulting from cult-like behavior is not as obvious as that headlined in the newspapers. Our own cult story is much less pronounced, with no noticeable beginning and no end; our perceptions, beliefs, and critical judgments are affected nonetheless.

We Americans live in a constitutional democracy, priding ourselves on the freedoms we have achieved. We live, travel and work without internal passports; we have free choice of job or profession; we may hold any belief and, within wide limits, do anything, say anything, write anything, and protest anything. We choose our governing officials from a list we have ourselves determined.

Democracy is based on an "eye-level" world in which we look directly at each other; every citizen is a peer. Political power is delegated, not inherited, not taken, not given by divine right, but bestowed by each of us. However, I believe that a danger exists even in democracies that the omnipresent authoritarian impulse will manifest itself in disguised form, will lead us toward a world in which we are always looking up at those who must be obeyed or down at those who must obey us. This is so because authoritarianism draws its strength from the same source that supports cult behavior: dependency on groups and leaders.

I believe that we need to bring into awareness the unconscious motivations and excluded information that influence our behavior and thought at the personal, national, and international levels. This requires that we first understand the dynamics of obvious cults and then address similar processes in ourselves and in ordinary society. Such understanding can provide us with tools for detecting cult behavior—our own as well as that of others—and enable us to step outside the cult circle.

I will begin with the history of a group which evolved into an extreme cult. The story is told by two of the group's converts, a real couple who underwent the experiences chronicled, although all the names used in my account are fictional and other changes have been made in their story.

"Hugh and Clara Robinson" were members of the cult for nearly a decade. Their story is significant because what they began in joy ended in terror and pain, their own relationship almost destroyed. The progression from heaven to hell was gradual, the steps of the descent justified in the name of God and said to be required if the group were to save the world, as they came to believe they could. The Robinsons' history is also significant because they were an intelligent, well-educated, normal couple—yet they came to believe in evil forces and in a group soul that could hold their own souls captive. Prior to their departure from the cult they and other members were spending as many as sixteen hours a day conducting one another through rites of "cleansing," exorcism, and the warding-off of devils. It may be difficult for the reader to identify with the Robinsons in this final, bizarre phase, but their story is classic and their vulnerability is shared by everyone to a greater extent than we realize.

Hugh and Clara escaped; others have not. Although it is important that we know about cults to avoid being caught in them, it is even more important that we study such groups to become aware of the hidden cult thinking operating unnoticed in our daily lives. Cults are mirrors of ourselves.

Hugh and Clara:
A Case History

WHEN Hugh and Clara Robinson joined Life Force it was an open, friendly, informal gathering of people who had become interested in the teachings of a charming man, Thomas Correll, a psychologist who lived in England and whom many of the group had visited. Correll met with whomever wanted to consult him, functioning more like a teacher than a traditional psychotherapist. He had developed a system of philosophy and techniques—life force psychology—designed to bring about psychotherapeutic change and personality growth. The sophistication of the theory, the effectiveness of the techniques, the sweetness and joy emanating from the man and, in particular, his emphasis on the spiritual combined to make Correll, and what he taught, very attractive to the highly educated, psychologically oriented men and women, mostly in their twenties and thirties, who began to meet together to carry on and promote his work.

The Robinsons had first encountered life force psychology when they participated in a workshop led by a very dedicated couple, Alex and Barbara Monroe. During that weekend, Hugh and Clara were guided in individual fantasies that were like dream journeys, and for the Robinsons the results were uplifting beyond their expectations.

CLARA: I had the experience of feeling more loved and accepted than I'd ever felt in my whole life. It was a real downflow of energy within me, just amazing. I had the feeling that this was something that I'd always wanted, that I had been looking outside myself for—and there it was.

HUGH: I had a very deep personal experience, realizing that I wasn't alone, that there were other people who cared about the same things I did. So I felt a brotherhood among these people.

After this experience the Robinsons wanted to learn more. They took several courses of study with the Monroes, traveled abroad to study with Thomas Correll for a few months, and decided to devote themselves full-time to studying and teaching life force psychology.

At that time Clara Robinson was over thirty, married, the mother of a young child. She had a bachelor's degree in English literature and had completed additional graduate work as well. Clara's relationships with her parents, siblings, and peers had been good. A leader in both high school and college, she was superior in intelligence and socially adept.

Clara's involvement with the Life Force group was rooted in her sense of a special beauty in the world, a transcendent quality. When she was a little girl she spent a lot of time alone in nature. The trees and birds were a special source of delight, as was her perception that

> light was very nearby, a feeling of things being very beautiful, in a way that I never found too many people to share it with . . . I had that when my child was born, too: the miracle of life.

Except for one teacher, the first person she met with whom she could share that reality was her husband, Hugh. She remembers thinking, He knows the secret thing, too. This shared sense of a greater reality was a central theme to their relationship. Clara wondered why more people didn't have that feeling of special beauty.

Later, life force psychology provided a way of understanding that experience. For the first time Clara could share her perception with others, could integrate this secret, precious part of herself into her life in a beneficial way. She found a way to express herself and to teach principles and techniques that she believed could help others as well.

The system answered other needs as well. After Clara and Hugh were married, they discovered the human potential movement and Clara joined a therapy group that unleashed a great deal of fear in her. Her anxiety became progressively worse, and psychotherapy did not help. At this point in her life Clara encountered the Monroes and had her initial "transformation session," a profound and exhilarating experience, convincing her that the transformation process—as taught by Alex and Barbara—would provide the help she was seeking.

The experience took place in a group setting. Clara had volunteered to work on her fear; "In those days I would do anything to get help." Alex Monroe asked, "What are you afraid of?"

CLARA: I'm afraid I will float away.

ALEX: Can you see what you are afraid you will float away from?

CLARA: No, but I know what it is—it's myself as a grown woman.

ALEX: Can you see her?

CLARA: And then I saw this really wonderful, grounded Earth Mother . . . like an enormous earthy woman . . . the opposite of my kind of thin, wispy, mystic identification. And I cried and cried and cried. It was just wonderful. And he [Alex] worked with that in dialog and imagery and then he said, "There's a wise old man in the sun" and so I went up toward the sun and there was this wise man and he said to me, "My child," and I climbed in his lap, like a child—he was very much like a father, as I retell it I realize that—I just felt like I was home. I felt a downflow of love and affection that I have never felt before or since . . . like being totally okay. This must be what I have always been looking for . . . "I'm really all right" . . . It was *very* important . . . like this big sigh in it . . . I could rest. It was that experience that made me feel that I needed to do more of whatever this system was.

Alex told her she could think of that wise person any time she wanted. Afterwards Clara did that and it helped calm her, as did visualizing the earth mother. This vivid experience of what I

would interpret as the dependency dream was profoundly important to Clara. "It felt like unconditional love, being totally accepted." She felt it had spiritual connotations as well. Clara
thought everyone must want and should have this acceptance.

Hugh was also over thirty when he joined Life Force. He had
studied at Princeton and was working on a Ph.D. in psychology.
Like Clara, he had good relationships with his family and was
close to his father and mother whom he described as spiritual
people although not formally religious; "They were just committed to making changes for a better world." His father and mother
both worked for liberal causes.

Throughout his school years Hugh had been an outstanding
student and leader, yet he felt isolated from his peers. There was
an artistic, sensitive side to himself that he was unable to share.
Hugh appeared strong, confident, and successful in studies and
athletics. He was a musician, popular with women, and the leader
of his class. Inside, however, he felt alone, missing the security of
his home environment where the spiritual part of himself was
shared and supported. He strongly associates this spiritual aspect
of his life with his love of music; when asked about early mystical
experiences he refers to his artistic side.

I had this intense, private spiritual life which I had always experienced in terms of music . . . what I would call supercon-
scious experiences . . . and then at age nineteen, in the Rock-
ies in Colorado, I had a spontaneous experience of unity with
everything. That never left, in a way. I think that was always
a backdrop to my searching.

This sense of the spiritual Hugh felt unable to share with his
friends. Looking back, he recognizes that his peers' jealousy of his
accomplishments added to his sense of isolation, "so there was
this mixture of not feeling really connected but yet being admired
by them and being a leader."

In college Hugh had a few good friends but felt even more like
a loner. He was disillusioned with the pretensions of academic life
and ceased trying to achieve the top.

At the time he encountered Life Force, Hugh was

ripe for something to believe in, to put my energy into . . . I
had a wife and child and I didn't feel too comfortable with

what it meant to be in the world and make a living. I was anxious about my life and wasn't sure that it was going to work out. I'd had to leave thing after thing because somehow it didn't satisfy me.

During that first workshop with the Monroes, Alex conducted Hugh in a long fantasy in which he climbed a mountain. At one point Alex suggested that Hugh become a beautiful tree that had been created in the fantasy. He did so.

There was this wonderful flow of energy, of roots and light . . . very powerful. I had never experienced anything like this before.

Alex then suggested that he leave the tree, continue on up the mountain, and then look at the sun.

Out of the sun came this figure and he came down . . . Greek, with a Franciscan robe on . . . a marvelous black beard, sort of green eyes . . . very alive and powerful figure and he just looked at me and we embraced and there was this wonderful feeling between us. Then we threw our arms around each other and we said, "Let's take on the world!" There was this sense that we were going to work together to help the rest of the world.

The guided fantasy went on for about an hour. At the end of it, Hugh opened his eyes. The original group of twenty-five had been reduced to four in addition to Alex and Barbara. It was midnight. Two of those who stayed had met Hugh previously, two had not.

They were all men . . . this was overwhelming to me, it was as powerful as the daydream . . . these people had stayed to be with me during this thing. Here were people who were sticking by me and not abandoning me for not understanding. And then Barbara said to me, "You don't have to be alone anymore." I just wept and wept . . . that I didn't have to be alone anymore.

Hugh and Clara shared an intuitive sense of a larger reality that was very important to them. However, I believe that this perception was confused with unresolved dependency longings that led them to interpret the guided daydream as spiritual and to accept the Monroes as guides or agents in that domain. Their enthusiasm for the new system was also due to its affirmation of their perceptions of the numinous world, perceptions which had not been acceptable to their peers. Suddenly, they found meaning, purpose, and helpful work to do.

The procedures and theoretical system of life force psychology had been put together by Thomas Correll, who had taught the Monroes when they had visited him four years before. Alex and Barbara were Correll's chief disciples, seemingly modeled after him in gentleness and altruism and in the loving attention they paid to those who came to learn and be helped by the system. They were totally dedicated to bringing this wonderful new teaching to others, to the world they believed needed it so badly.

Over the next four years life force psychology became popular, numerous workshops were given, and training sessions were developed for mental health professionals. The Robinsons had many sessions with the Monroes and received personal instruction abroad from Correll, as did almost all those who joined the Life Force group at the initial stage. Soon Clara and Hugh began to lead workshops and training sessions, moving to be near the Monroes so they could be more involved in the work. They felt they had the life they had always wanted. The spiritual values formerly split off from their working lives were now directly expressed and shared with a group of peers to whom they felt connected, people who validated and gave support to each other.

Hugh could now put his leadership abilities to use for a cause he believed in. He was appointed to the executive committee of the Life Force Psychology Center and conducted workshops and training sessions all over the United States. The theory of life force psychology particularly appealed to him.

> I loved the ideas, I loved the system . . . It felt like the most comprehensive and humane way of looking at people I'd found. I could work with these ideas about human nature that fit with how [I felt] when I played music or studied literature or whatever . . . There was just a very deep personal connection. It was mental as well as emotional . . . like being on a frontier. There was a tremendous amount of excitement and intellectual stimulation . . .

For Clara also, life force psychology and Life Force (the group) fulfilled important needs and involved her deepest feelings.

It really fit with what I valued, what I had always hoped for. I must always have been a closet mystic, I suppose . . . suddenly there was a form [for the spiritual] and there was someone teaching who said you can work with people this way. So I gradually got more involved in teaching, in designing workshops. I was doing work with women at that time and there was quite a lot of freedom in the beginning to do my own thing. The workshops were attended and they grew and my confidence in teaching grew.

The members of the Life Force Psychology Center supported and encouraged her teaching.

What was exciting for me was that there was a place for my spiritual experience within the psychological system and I could learn to work with people to evoke that, and have them trust that and tap into it . . . learning how to help people get in touch with more love and compassion and with their creativity. I think *affirming* is the best word I could use. It just felt like it was affirming the best in people.

Gradually, this sense of high purpose gave rise to feelings of specialness which later led to the devaluation of those outside the group and to the elevation of Alex.

CLARA: [During these early years] there was a growing sense that this group was special and that we were doing something special that nobody else was . . . and that Alex was special.

The Robinsons were happy with their teaching role in Life Force. Five satisfying years went by. They conducted therapy sessions, taught workshops and classes. They believed that what they were doing was making a unique contribution to the world. Hugh in particular felt this to be a time of growth and personal fulfillment. He was an executive of the Center and, at the same time, had good friends in other professional organizations devoted to humanistic and spiritual concerns. He helped plan conferences, gave major presentations, traveled widely, and interacted with Life Force groups in other countries. Thus, for a long time there was a balance between Hugh's involvement with the

Life Force Psychology Center and the rest of the world of humanistic and transpersonal psychology.

Clara engaged in similar activities, although to a lesser extent.
She divided her life between Center work and her family. While
Life Force took up a large part of her time and energy, she felt a
reasonable share remained for her son and Hugh. Clara and Hugh
were both pleased with the way their lives were going, convinced
that Life Force was making a unique and vital contribution to the
world.

Then the Center moved to better offices in the city and expanded teaching activities in other parts of the country and to
Europe. With that move, the Robinson's life and that of the others
in the group became more and more conflicted, painful, and distorted. More time was demanded from each member. This demand was made by Alex Monroe at a meeting of the executive
committee, which transmitted it to a larger meeting that included
the other members of the group (such as Clara). Pressure for compliance with this and other demands was usually from the group
as a whole although Alex would personally exert extra pressure,
if needed, on a balky member.

Clara experienced most of her conflicts with the Life Force
group over the issue of commitment to her family. There was a
competition for time and energy between the group and her son.

> I dragged my heels [against an increased commitment to the
> group] . . . There was a meeting where we were all supposed
> to make a commitment to take the work of the Center further.
> I was the last to, as they put it, "put my sword on the table." I
> said, "I'm not sure I can do it, I'm not sure it's really right for
> me."

Finally Clara agreed. Such conflicts were continual, but she
told herself that giving increasing time to the Center was right
because it was needed.

> Everyone around me seems to think it's okay . . . all these rea-
> sons. Somehow I let it be all right, I told myself it was all right,
> even though I didn't feel good about it. There were lots of
> things like that. The first impulse would be, This isn't right.
> And then someone questions it . . . maybe it's me or maybe
> it's someone else . . . and they get really put down. Sometimes

there would be an awful silence in the room, sometimes it could be twenty people all looking at you incredulously and someone saying, "How could you worry about that? Don't you see that we really need to . . ." There wasn't any opening for a different point of view; there was no space for other opinions . . . I told myself it must be right, but I don't think I ever stopped hearing that voice, saying it was not right.

Thus the group enforced compliance and dissent was stifled. Over the next few years, questionable practices, introduced by Alex, gradually increased, requiring further suppression of the members' sense of what was right. One such incident concerned a publicity write-up for Clara's workshops.

There was a real effort to puff up the write-ups [make them look more impressive] . . . I had taught several night courses at the university but they wanted to put down that I had taught at the university itself. I remember questioning it and when you would question, from all sides there would come, "Why were you thinking that? This is an opportunity to get our work more known . . ." There would be a response that made me feel like I couldn't keep pushing for it. I backed down a lot . . . "Clara! How could you suggest that!" was the message. Alex would say, "Here we are doing such important work and you let that bother you? What a petty little thing to be concerned with."

A great deal of "psychotherapeutic processing" among Center members took place over the telephone. When the issue was taping phone conversations, Alex (as always) had many justifications.

CLARA: Incredible, elaborate reasons, sometimes reasons you just couldn't understand, they were so complicated. The idea was that if we have a record of phone calls between people if something goes wrong we can have a record and then look and see whose fault it was or what the problem was . . . [As far as outside phone calls were concerned,] Well, by then the outside world was the enemy and so we wanted to know exactly what happened.

Eventually, Alex asked them to tape everything.

CLARA: I really encountered my ability to rationalize. If I had paid attention to all those occasions when everything inside of me said, "No, this isn't right," I couldn't have stayed there. If I had really taken a stand, let's say on the taping, and said, "I will not go along with this," first of all, it would have taken a kind of strength that I don't know I had at the time because everyone in the room [would be saying] "Clara, you want to have dinner with your son? You're so selfish . . ." I would have had to be willing to stand there and have everyone in the room say "No."

Thus, the group enforced compliance by the use of rhetoric that exploited Clara's idealism for the group's own purposes. Alex led the way. If he was opposed on grounds of principle, Alex attacked those principles by equating them with selfish desires. The members had doubts about Alex's reasoning, but they never really discussed the matter among themselves out of fear that Alex might learn of it. Sometimes, after a meeting, members would walk home together and say, "God, that was weird, wasn't it?"

CLARA: We would sneak those little things to each other. But you could never be sure that that person wouldn't get home and call Alex and say, "Boy, Clara Robinson was really identifying with her desire nature. You should have heard what Clara said after the meeting."

This suspicion extended to close friends.

I couldn't even be sure that Hugh wouldn't do that; I did that on him. There was no safe person to trust with that intuitive sense [of something being wrong] . . . You couldn't be sure . . . sometimes someone else would say, "Yeah, I didn't like that, either," but you didn't know if that would be kept in confidence. There was no one but yourself to corroborate. If someone coming home had said . . . if we had said together, "It isn't right, what happened to so-and-so . . ." Any of that would have made a tremendous difference—there was none.

So dissent was silenced. Typically, Alex did not demand that members inform on each other; rather, they were asked to provide information that could be used to "help" the other person.

CLARA: It used to be a way of getting in with Alex. He was always glad for that information. I remember the first time I was asked to give [information] . . . Alex said, "I'm going to bring this thing up about Jerry and if you could share that piece in the meeting that would be very helpful." I remember [saying] "I'm not sure that is right," but then the rationale would be that it would really help Jerry and I'd say, "Oh, that's right, Jerry can learn from that if he can see that; that will really help him." A lot of things went under that reasoning— a lot of bad things. Then there were times when people would volunteer . . . getting Alex's favor was a pretty important thing, particularly toward the end, getting his approval . . . He definitely had real favorites and they'd change. It was never a very secure favoritism, you could lose it at any point.

Hugh's experience was similar. Like the others, he wished for Alex's approval, and fear of losing it led him to compromise his principles and avoid dissent.

HUGH: There were things that were beginning to happen there that I was uncomfortable about. But because my personal connection had been so deep, I kept saying, "It's worth it. This work is so good, it's so effective, that I'll overlook . . ." Alex lied. Just little things, like changing the date on a letter, but I hated that. And I would say, "Why do we have to do that?" and he would have some quick answer that would say why it was necessary, because someone would screw him if he didn't, basically. And so I said, O.K. . . . And then it was lying to people about different situations [in order to control them]. The Executive Committee would get together and plan exactly what was going to go in the meeting, what was going to happen, so that there was no trust of the natural caring or power or whatever in people in the Center. But because the work was so "good," you know, I loved it, I turned a blind eye. Every year, I'd think, "Something's not right here. And yet, something is so right here." We pushed away a lot of stuff . . . that's what we realize, now, but we didn't at the time.

Alex's power derived from the assumption that he knew much more than the others about the teaching and thus was entitled to special authority. Indeed, it turned out that there had been a secret, mystical side to Thomas Correll that only some knew about, a deep involvement in an esoteric group devoted to occult writings. Correll had given occult books to Alex, who eventually began to teach his own version of the elaborate esoteric system to an inner circle at the Center, those people whom he felt to be most committed to the work.

HUGH: I thought Alex was smarter than me, more evolved, because he knew all this occult stuff . . . [he would] use chapter and verse to rationalize these things. It was like a priest using a Bible. He read it much more than anyone else and no one could refute it.

Thomas Correll died. The Robinsons later recalled that Alex had begun making disparaging comments about Correll prior to the man's death, remarking that he was too vague, too lax, too generous with his time, too indiscriminate, not focused enough, something of a fuddy-duddy. After Correll's death, such comments were more frequent. Alex became the only source of the teaching, the one who determined whether others would or would not continue to receive its benefits. Barbara Monroe became more and more subordinate. As Alex gradually exerted more and more control over the group's other members, their dependence on him increased. While he claimed to work and share power with the executive committee, in fact he subtly retained all power and control in his own hands. The committee soon realized that their job was to discuss and debate until they reached the decision Alex wanted. Alex did not acknowledge what he was doing and maintained the facade of democracy for a long time after it had become perfectly obvious to the others that he was the sole authority.

Clara's request for enough time to be with her child was labeled a selfish desire by the group. She recalls that there had never been any respect for her role as a mother. There was constant pressure on her to comply with the group's demand for more and more time. First, it was all mornings and then it was mornings and two afternoons, then five, and then meetings on Saturday as well.

CLARA: "Clara, when you really get it that your family is the whole world then you'll understand that David is just one of the many children you are responsible for." When we were asked to take the Center another step, I dragged my heels. There was this noise in my head: "Should I do this? Shouldn't I do this? Maybe it will be wrong and then what?" I remember at one point saying, "I'll do it", and everything got quiet around me and the noise in my head stopped and I thought, "God, maybe that is right. What I am being asked to do is to make a fuller commitment to this good work . . ." And inside me I thought the quiet or sense of rightness means I'm doing the right thing to get more involved.

After several months of commuting to the new Center, the Robinsons moved to the city. The pressure on group members to give totally of their time and energy became overwhelming.

HUGH: By that time we were working six or seven days a week . . . leaving at six o'clock in the morning and coming back whenever. We had two cars and sometimes we had to drive separately . . . what that did was to fragment our family life.

Hugh was having a harder and harder time maintaining balance in his professional life as well. His involvements outside the Center drew increasing fire from Alex and the inner circle. He had never been one of Alex's favorites. On the few occasions when Alex had tried to use him as a confidant to help deal with another member, Hugh had felt very uncomfortable and failed the task. On occasions when Hugh disagreed, Alex justified everything with arguments and by citing the occult books. Hugh's rebellions against Alex's control were always short-lived.

I would kick up a fuss and then I would give in, that's the pattern. "All for the good" . . . he would get me on the "good." "Oh, I see, for that reason, because it's spiritually right." There was always a host of reasons that would evoke my caring for the cause and then I'd go along with it rather than saying, "Look! The cause is being violated right here!"

When Hugh asserted the importance of his family's needs, Alex would say,

Hugh, if your family was starving and you had one pound of wheat, would you make bread for your family or would you plant it to feed the starving million?

This appeal to higher purpose, to the greater good, was Alex's stock in trade, and was copied by the group when it needed to pressure uncooperative members.

HUGH: It didn't quite fit but I had to go along with it because intellectually it made sense. I would discount my strong feelings. Everything was to be sacrificed to the greater, the larger: bringing Life Force into people's lives . . . I never won a battle; it was just a matter of how long I could stand up to it before it became too painful and then I would let myself be persuaded and would give in. [But] then I would subvert the system by just going right out and doing what I was doing.

The executive committee attacked Hugh's outside activities.

This allegation of evil began to come at me . . . that I was identified with my "elemental" [selfish nature] and so forth . . . More and more it would be that I had done something wrong and I had to fix it and I would try. Every time I would return from a committee meeting [of an outside organization] to the Executive Committee of the Center I was called on the carpet for doing power trips, for not telling them everything that happened, for not getting Alex on the [conference] program. So I felt increasingly at odds but I was confused and wanted to do the right thing . . . [I was] torn between my loyalties . . . torn to pieces.

Alex planned to establish a graduate school of life force psychology with branches in North and South America and in Europe. It was a very ambitious project and required even more time and effort from group members. The actual establishment of the first of these graduate schools in the city, after the group moved there, was a pivotal event, one which inspired a further intensification of the cult process. Anyone who questioned the direction of the group was seen as an enemy who needed to be controlled or pushed down, whether the questioner was a group member or an outsider. As a result, members became more and more isolated from colleagues in other human service organizations and their time and energy were even more tightly controlled.

Abruptly, Hugh was removed from his position on the executive committee. At a meeting of that body he was told he was not contributing to the "group mind," asked to leave the executive committee's circle and discontinue almost all activities at the graduate school, where he had been teaching. He was instead given the lowest, least important assignments and asked to teach beginning workshops. Much of his time was spent cataloging cassette tapes and xeroxing. Occasionally, when he was allowed to teach a course at the graduate school, his proposal would be severely criticized.

> I became increasingly filled with fear and self-doubt . . . fear of what the group could do to me, fear of hurt, of rejection; fear of somehow being alone again. I was very alone and had lost whatever fellowship I had in the earlier years that had drawn me toward the group . . . turned against by people within the Executive group that I cared about.

At the same time, Clara's loyalties were being drawn away from Hugh towards the group. Lewis, Hugh's close friend, was echoing the group's abuse. Hugh was afraid of being abandoned completely. The isolation he thought he had left behind by joining Life Force now had reappeared within it.

> I was afraid of being alone, afraid of being cast out of Eden . . . even though Eden had turned into Hell . . . afraid of being cast out even further. There was still, "Well, we're doing the graduate school, Hugh, and you can't think, so you can do these other things and we'll still be nice to you and we won't tell other people that you are no longer an Executive." In other words, there was still "caring" for me and I was still grasping for any care I could get.

For Clara, also, Eden was turning into hell. Not only did she experience an increasingly painful struggle to meet her son's needs, but her relationship with Hugh came under attack. One evening, late at night, she was called to meet with several executive committee members with whom she had warm ties. They told her that Hugh was having trouble and that they were having trouble with him.

> Hugh has been asked not to be on the Executive and we just want you to know that we really value you . . . we want you to stay no matter what happens . . . we want you to know that we really trust what you do.

Lewis offered further reassurance.

> LEWIS: Clara, if anything happens, you can come to my house and bring your kid.

CLARA: That always happened whenever anything was done to a couple; the other member of the couple would get a lot of attention: "You're different . . . you're special," whatever . . .

These men whom I cared about made a real effort to get me to stand with them in their condemnation of him [Hugh] and to see him with their eyes. I betrayed our bond in that time . . . there was always truth [in the accusations], there were seeds of truth . . . there was stuff in me that both wanted to hear and also saw some of the things they were saying. And that part of me that was always dependent on Hugh was delighted to get that much attention from these men in the group, just delighted . . . and support for my teaching and all that came after that time . . . That was just one of those times that I betrayed Hugh and betrayed the bond we had from all those years together.

The meeting with these men had been carefully planned by Alex, and he had met with them earlier to lay out the strategy they were to use on Clara.

The splitting of couples was one of the most malignant and prominent features of Alex's tyranny, the foundation whereby he established and increased his control over the members of Life Force. The support and reality testing provided a given member by his or her trusted partner was subverted; ties and loyalty that supported his or her sense of self-worth were compromised. The guilt experienced may have provided substance to charges later on that the couple harbored evil forces, accusations hurled at them by Alex, the person orchestrating their mutual betrayal.

This direct attempt to split the Robinsons capitalized on the erosion that had already taken place in their relationship. Ever-increasing demands on their time left almost no opportunity for them to be together. "Circles of silence," the structure of secrecy that Alex established, further weakened their relationship. The executive committee did not share what happened at their meetings with the senior members, those at the next level down. They, in turn, withheld information from those below them, the members, who did not share with the students. Finally, in the year before the graduate school opened, Hugh and the other executive committee members were asked to take a formal vow of secrecy. Hugh was not to confide in Clara, as he had been doing. As he had done with similar matters in the past, Hugh protested, struggled, but then yielded to the pressure. When he was thrown off the executive committee he was not able to share what had happened with his wife, nor did she confide in him about what had been said to her.

A few months went by before Clara also found herself in trouble. She was said to have "bad energy." This time it was Hugh who was asked to cooperate with the group in dealing with her. When he went out of town to teach they persuaded him to leave Clara a note saying that he wouldn't have any contact with her during the ten days that he would be away. Soon after, they put Clara in "quarantine."

Quarantine was a procedure of restricting a member to his or her house or apartment, having contact with no one except Alex or one other executive that Alex might designate. Quarantined members were supposed to reflect upon their "bad energy" or "power trips" or their "elemental" (basic evil)—whatever fault had been detected by Alex. They waited until a phone call came, which might mean being "processed" for hours by Alex or an executive until they saw the error of their ways.

> HUGH: I remember waiting fourteen hours for a phone call in total panic, and it turned out the Executive Committee had decided not to call me and had gone to bed . . . and I was sitting there, waiting.

The period of quarantine was one of acute deprivation lasting days or months. To an outsider, there would seem to be no reason for a member to put up with it. To understand, one must recognize that despite the negative aspects of Life Force, there were also times when the members laughed together, when the entire group was close and caring, times when they shared food and felt a love for each other that seemed genuine and precious. In quarantine, all this was withdrawn.

> HUGH: People who a day before you had been laughing with, having fun with, working with, would just turn their eyes away; they wouldn't even make eye contact. If you have the experience of love and then you're cut off from it, there's a tremendous motivation to get back to it, tremendous desire to reconnect with that love . . . And you'll do anything to get

back because it makes you feel good . . . makes you feel you're a good person.

The effort to split the Robinsons continued. When Clara fell from grace, Hugh was exhorted to stand up to her, to "be a man!" Hugh later recalled a particular moment when Alex said, "Hugh, we want you to own your power."

HUGH: For just a minute I had a perception of Hell . . . I saw a devil's face . . . red, everything. It was a perception that the totally opposite thing was happening than what he was saying. I saw that this was Hell . . . and then it [the perception] went again. I rationalized and said, "He wants me to own my power so I am going to go stand up to Clara." I couldn't. I came back from England—she'd been isolated ten days—she met me at the door . . . she was in tears. I came and sat with her and we had a good talk . . . [later] I told Alex and the others that we'd talked and I got lambasted for giving in, for being manipulated by her tears. [They said] that I should have been tough and told her to cut out the bullshit. Well, I didn't.

Following the establishment of the graduate school, Alex had placed more and more stress on "the elemental", which he defined as evil, selfishness, the opposite of spirituality, the anti-Christ. This concept came from the esoteric system the group had studied, but Alex magnified it until protecting the group from evil—from within and without—became the major focus of the group's activities. Members who opposed him were said to be yielding to their selfish side, identifying with it, harming the group and themselves through its influence. Although not directly stated, the implied message was that the only hope to free themselves from their own evil lay in Alex's guidance. As Clara recalled, the message was, If you don't watch out, if you don't look, if you don't see evil, if you don't listen to me, you will be caught in eternal hell.

The ultimate in devaluation was directed against anyone who left the group. They were declared to have completely given in to their elemental, their selfishness, their badness; and whatever had been good in them, their soul itself, was said to have been left behind in the group. Such people were shunned as contaminating forces, they were declared to have turned against their own souls.

CLARA: Once you left, they didn't speak to you again. They passed you on the street without speaking, even though you'd been with them for years . . . There was a feeling toward the end that you ought to be careful of who you got involved with, because you could lose anyone at any minute. Someone you really loved might just go or . . . get bad, so don't get too involved. Anyone you saw as good might flip [become bad] any day . . . your husband, your best friend . . . that's a strange feeling.

Alex was feared because he could judge someone to be bad and the rest of the group would go along. Dissent was invariably punished.

CLARA: When he would say, "Mary is selfish," we could usually pick out things that would support that. Your seeing would be affected by it: "Oh yeah! I remember when I had lunch with her last week . . ." And you'd take an incident that in another setting you might not notice, but you could pull them out . . . particularly if you wanted to get in with him at that moment, you would look for those times. You'd certainly not say, "I haven't seen that; that hasn't been my experience." Boy! If you disagreed with how Alex was seeing it you were in deep trouble. The times I did were invariably used against me, if not at the moment, then later.

Opposition of any kind would call forth processing so that the member could see that he or she had been giving in to their selfish nature. Such experiences could be devastating:

CLARA: I had two experiences of being in a large group where I was on the spot for supposedly not being a good person, with about eighteen people—my "friends"—bringing up information about why I wasn't a good person. I don't think I've ever been through anything so awful in my life, but I bought it . . . I think that in some funny way those meetings were usually triggered by a time when a person was seeing that something was wrong . . . being "difficult" . . . When Alex said, "We're going to have three . . . campuses, continue the Journal of Life Force Psychology and start a training program to compete [with independent Life Force groups in other cities] . . . ," I said, "How can we possibly do this?" My question was met with stony silence from the whole group. Erica worked with me three or four hours the next day to let me see that that was my elemental that had asked that question—not just my common sense!

Coupled with the emphasis on evil was Alex Monroe's growing interest and belief in past lives, a theory of reincarnation at the group level. Alex told the executive committee that they had all been together in many past lives and he had them play out past-life scenarios. One of the first past lives was called the Persian Past Life. Alex was a priest in ancient Persia; Hugh was a king and there was a church-state conflict. Everyone had a part. Typically, Alex did not need to specify the others' roles. Patricia, another member (whom Hugh had been trying to protect from criticism by the executive committee) became his sister. The priest, Alex, burned Patricia at the stake; thus the group fantasy translated events happening within the group into terms of past lives.

Alex's control over the Life Force members' lives increased further. Each day they were supposed to fill out time sheets detailing every activity conducted throughout the day. Although most hated this, the procedure was rationalized as improving efficiency and it soon became an instrument of control. The sheets were often collected and looked over when a member was thought to be a problem; then there would be a meeting with one or more of the executive committee who would take the errant person to task. Meeting with people outside the group required the permission of the executive committee. Behind them, controlling everything, was Alex.

Supporting Alex's power, keeping the members committed to the organization, no matter how bizarre their lives became, was the shared belief that they were a special group, doing work of great importance to the world.

CLARA: I think in the end, [we believed that] we were the only people doing this . . . and I remember thinking, "Isn't this strange that [our little group] sitting around could be this special group." I think we had the feeling that Alex was an important articulator of the Christ or the coming of the Christ . . . I think he believed that more and more himself.

Hugh's behavior continued to be "bad" and he was placed under surveillance. When he went to Baltimore to conduct a workshop, Margaret, one of the executive committee, accompanied and supervised him. Hugh's mother and father lived in Baltimore, but he was not allowed to stay with them. Instead, he checked into a motel. When he did visit his parents, Margaret went with him.

Hugh's brother was involved in the Baltimore Life Force group and a few months after Hugh's visit there trouble developed.

HUGH: Alex used his power to split up the Baltimore group and my brother became the evil one there. Alex got three of the people to put him and a friend out in twenty-four hours . . . telling them they couldn't come to their office . . . a kind of strong arm job which was tremendously upsetting to my brother because his friends with whom he had built this thing turned against him. My mother got very upset, understandably, and called up one of her friends [in the Center] who she knew and said, "What is going on there?"

As far as Alex was concerned, this intervention by Hugh's mother made her a source of evil.

HUGH: I went to lunch with Alex and some of the other Executives and he said that evil energy was coming from my mother toward the group so I was going to have to cut off from her. I remember feeling this terror because I had seen this happen in other situations and I said, "Oh, my God, it's coming here." But again, I was immobilized, filled with fear and self-doubt, afraid to resist. We did a long session that afternoon, I connected with the Christ . . . Alex used the thing of . . . Christ says, "You have to leave your father and your mother in order to follow me" . . . I bought it and although I again had this terribly ambivalent feeling of disorientation and confusion and being in over my head, yet, at the same time being too afraid to disagree and, so, I felt I had to go along with it.

Hugh wrote to his parents expressing anger at them for criticizing the organization, telling them that what happened in Baltimore had nothing to do with his group. His parents wrote back letters of apology which Alex read. For a moment, Alex was moved by the letters and admitted that they were very beautiful. Then, a half-hour later, he declared the letters were "too perfect." Hugh was ordered to "cut" from his mother as well as from his brother. This demand was made despite the fact that during that period, Hugh's brother was ill, diagnosed as having cancer. What had been oppressive control by the group and Alex was becoming horrific.

The horror can best be sensed by visualizing the procedure of "cutting," which was practiced more and more in the later phase of the group. Cutting was a process in which members separated themselves from whomever had been declared a source of evil energy—a friend, lover, parent, husband, or wife. They were to visualize cords stretching from their heart to the heart of the other person. Then they were instructed to cut the cords. Sometimes they would go a step further and "burn the image," visualizing the person being consumed by flames. Later, when Clara reflected on all that happened, the cutting she had done was one of the things that was still painful, about which she felt most ashamed.

> I feel I betrayed myself at these times, I let myself do that . . . on some level it didn't seem right, it felt wrong . . . We asked about it, "Why was this necessary?" Alex would say, "Well, it's not really them that you're burning, it's your projection of them." I feel sad that I did that . . . that one feels really hard to live with.

Hugh discontinued all communication with his parents. His brother became more and more ill, but phone calls from the brother went unanswered. During this time Clara was increasingly critical of Hugh, seeing him as identified with his elemental, accepting Alex's evaluation of him and believing, with the group, that his refusal to speak to his family was correct, although difficult. The rest of the group also supported his action and rewarded him with positive attention.

> HUGH: I got a lot of reinforcement from it which reinforced my desire to get back into the group . . . here were these people approving of me cutting off my parents . . . But there was a lot of dread and not wanting to go on, [not knowing] how we could get out of this nightmare. But I didn't know how to get out short of leaving and that didn't cross my mind. I guess by that time I knew that if I left I would have lost Clara and David [their son].

Hugh's sister visited him and told him that their brother was worse and that his parents were desperately trying to get through

to him, calling the Center repeatedly, but being put off. Hugh
called Debbie, one of Alex's inner circle, and told her something
must be done. It was agreed that Hugh would phone his brother
but that the call would be taped and monitored by Alex and
Debbie.

HUGH: Strangely enough, in the middle of all this chaos, my
brother and I sort of reached through to this place of connection between the two of us . . . talking about his dying, how
much we loved each other, how we cared . . . and I have this
tape which I listen to every once in a while.

About a week later, Alex worked on Clara to convince her to
tell Hugh to leave their house.

CLARA: Alex said Hugh's energy continued to be bad and I,
too, felt that he [Hugh] didn't seem good . . . and then, after
a meeting, with about ten other people watching . . . Alex
talked with me to the point of my deciding what was really
best for Hugh was for me to ask him to leave the house . . .
and I cried and cried and cried . . . it was very hard.

As soon as Clara agreed to tell Hugh to leave, something happened to her that seemed to validate the decision.

When I made that choice, I had a lot of energy coming in, I
mean literally . . . not only did everyone in the room say,
"Clara, you're so brave and I really support this and I see how
hard it is," but something happened in my head . . . I felt sort
of strong and full . . . I saw this happen to Mary . . . when
she chose to leave Bill, to stay in the group and let Bill quit . . .
the same kind of downflow happened . . . it is like some letting go and you get more energy . . .
I interpreted it inwardly, "Oh, not only do they say it is all
right but look what is happening to me!" I saw that again and
again . . . for instance when Margaret announced she was
leaving Fred, when Dick announced he was divorcing Connie
and was never going to see Connie and his children again—
that has got to be one of the worst stories in the whole group
. . . all those times those people looked big and shiny . . .
Margaret when she said, "I'm not going to be with Fred,"
looked as beautiful as I had ever seen her and inside of me I
went, "God, it must be right—look at her!"

Probably, what Clara and other members in such situations experienced was the effect of a sudden release from the intense conflict that was tearing at them, coupled with a child-like surrender, a letting go to the protection and power of the parent/family group. Later on, when he or she had finally left Life Force, the reality of what had been done became clear.

Clara experienced this letting-go phenomenon again when, a short time later, she was asked to break off communication with her own mother.

> I know this second hand. They said one night, "Clara has got to leave her mother"—that came up around the dinner table—so they called me down . . . They worked on me and worked on me and I just wouldn't budge on it. And Alex said, "Clara, I think you're asking Hugh to do something you're not willing to do." That was heavy and I realized that was probably true . . . and then he had me go up [in imagery] . . . there was a star we used to see and he said, "Ask the star what to do." Then, somehow, the star said something about "You need to let go of your mother and follow me" . . . or something like that. What happened was that again I got that really big hit of rightness . . . I cried and then, "Oh, that's right, I do need to do that." I remember at that moment Alex was saying, "If you do that, He [Christ] can take care of her too, help her more." And I said, "Oh, that's right." At that moment I thought I was loving her and that he [Alex] was, too.

Clara had her phone disconnected and changed her number so that her mother could no longer reach her. Her very perception of her mother was altered.

> When I was out of touch with my mother I would get letters from her. I would read them in the set [context] that she—or part of her—was trying to get me away from this work, trying to get me off my spiritual path. When you read a letter with that in your head it almost feels like there's [negative] energy in the letter. It's amazing because I've also seen those letters later, when it wasn't like that at all.

A week after Hugh made his last phone call to his dying brother, Clara told him to leave the house. He packed his bags and spent the night in a motel.

HUGH: It was the worst night of my life. I felt like I had lost everything. There was no Clara and David, no contact with group members, any family members. My only contact was with Alex and Debbie. I was totally surrounded in darkness. I did come through that night realizing two things: that light was important, spiritual light . . . and that giving was important.

A few weeks later, Hugh's brother died. His family had been sending telegrams as his condition worsened but Clara, having been told that Hugh did not want to see them, passed them on to the executive committee.

HUGH: By then, they had influenced her very much. I certainly felt betrayed by her, too. So my brother died and I didn't know when . . . that was one request I made to Alex and Debbie: that I would know the day he died. They wouldn't tell me because they said I was holding on to my brother. I found out that he had died a week or so after when my sister was threatening to come find me. So the Executive Committee had to do something, had to tell me. Otherwise, I don't think they would have.

Hugh continued in quarantine, having contact only with the executive committee. Several months after Clara asked him to leave the house, the group began pressing her to file for a divorce. She resisted, but eventually agreed and wrote to Hugh informing him of her decision. When she told her son David of the plan he became very upset, screamed, pounded on the floor and then ran out of the house. When he finally returned he phoned Alex's children, who were his friends. This created a disturbance in the Monroe household, with the result that Alex's wife Barbara had to be processed.

Alex had no sympathy for David's distress and interpreted his behavior as showing that David was elemental, that he was using his pain at his parents' separation to manipulate people. It was a theory of Alex's that when a child is born the mother sees the evil part of the baby but does not want to recognize it. He said that it was very important that the mother, in this case, Clara, be aware of the evil element in her child and teach him not to act on it. Alex told Clara to go to a special room at the Center where she could scream, pound pillows, and express rage at David, while he [Alex] guided the experience over the telephone. As standard procedure, a team of group members gathered in another location to support the processing by engaging in "subjective work," "cleaning up" Clara from contaminating influences.

CLARA: [They would be saying,] "Well, I see Clara connected with David, so let's cut Clara from David and let's burn David's image. Oh, and Clara is connected with Lewis, too, and Hugh. Let's clean her up (cut her from them).

Throughout the session, Alex kept insisting that Clara see the evil part in David.

CLARA: "I remember saying, "I don't want to see this, I don't want to see this." And Alex saying, tenderly, "Clara, it's all right, it's all right. He's just a boy trying to find his way." And I thought, "Oh, that's right." And, "You can help him, you can help him with it [the evil part] if you let yourself see it." I believed it for a few days . . . and Alex would tell me that I really needed to discipline David . . . there was a lot of stuff about David's evil part . . . it really pushed me to my limit.

After Hugh received Clara's letter asking for a divorce, he wrote back that he still wanted responsibility for his son, whom he hadn't seen in four months. He gave the letter to the executive committee, who kept it and did not give it to Clara.

CLARA: We came to fear and distrust each other. Hugh was afraid I was this awful way, and I was afraid he was the way Alex was telling me.

HUGH: We were taught to see the other as evil. Everybody began to see everybody else as predominantly this evil part, the part that was selfish and wanted to control people, that was separative, and so forth.

At this stage, to leave the group was a fearsome step because it meant, literally, to be damned.

HUGH: Increasingly, one's spiritual fate became identified with the group. So we all thought our souls were members of this group soul and that if you got taken over by your evil part you would be cut off from your soul. "This is the way to salvation and if you deviate in any way, you're siding with your evil part, you're identifying with it, you're making it bigger." If you thought about leaving the group you had to face the fact that in that system you'd be spiritually damned.

Members came to believe that without the help of Alex Monroe and the Life Force group, a person would have no chance of avoiding "the left-hand path," their evil side would overcome them despite their best intentions.

CLARA: It was never really said, but that was the implication . . . to leave meant to be eternally lost or caught, trapped in the selfish, comfort-seeking part of you that didn't care about the larger world, about alleviating suffering. We began to talk about it more and more and people who left were seen that way, "Poor Jennie, she just went to her selfishness." When we finally left that was the fear we had to struggle with.

Nevertheless, Clara did manage to leave the group, just three days before she was to start divorce proceedings against Hugh. At the time, she had been in quarantine again.

First when Hugh was in quarantine I was very much in favor and getting lots of attention . . . then I lost favor . . . I began to be seen as bad by Alex and a number of other people. One of them was Mary, a close friend. She turned me in to Alex and that was really the final straw . . .
    If Mary is going to see me this way, who else is there? I'm not with my husband; I'm out of contact with my parents; I'm making my son bad . . . and now Mary thinks I'm bad.

One morning Clara was told that the executive committee had some subjective work for her to do. For the first time, Clara refused. She was immediately told to cut from Lewis and Hal (who both had recently left the group) and two or three other members who were thought to be influencing her.

CLARA: I don't know if I even did it but I said that I need to take the day off . . . So I walked all day long and around where Hugh was living hoping I would run into him. I think that was the day that I began to consider going and to let that thought be a reality. The fact that Lewis and Hal had left already really influenced me. Leaving became an option in that universe, it suddenly became a possibility . . . something you could do . . . leaving exists . . . it was real . . . and it hadn't been up 'til then.

For Clara, the deciding issue was her son.

I sometimes thought . . . [what enabled me to leave] was the mother lion energy in me. It was like . . . "My husband, my parents and my friends, but not my baby . . . you just can't have him. I don't care if you're right about this, I'm not going to let you have him" . . . And that got me out of there as much as anything did. Alex was capturing every piece of my life, every relationship I had, every piece of my time . . . Oh, God! . . . capturing it and taking it into himself. I'm glad I had a child, that was the touchstone, although in the week before I left there was one moment when I considered I would give him up if Alex asked me to . . . I remember that thought coming into my head, "Am I really committed here? Would I give up my son if I was asked to?" And I thought maybe I would . . . other people have given up their children, so it isn't something that might not have happened.

That night she told a representative of the group that she wanted to stay but that she wanted three things: to have dinner with her son each night; to go to bed at midnight and get up at 7:00 instead of 3:00 or 4:00 (members of the group had been averaging from four to six hours of sleep for over a year); and to have some time for herself to swim and garden. She was challenged, "Clara, if you had to let go of those things for the group, would you do it?" Clara replied angrily, "I don't know why I should! I don't know why it has to be that way!" The response was, "Well, you'd better think about it some more."

That was the night, really. As soon as I hung up the phone I went upstairs and called a close friend who was outside the group. It happened very fast. She was someone who had been in a spiritual group. She had known Alex and something about Life Force, so I knew she'd be someone who would understand the spiritual commitment we had made; I didn't want to talk to someone who would be critical of all that . . .

She was wonderful. She didn't just say, "leave," or anything. It was like a little crack opened. I said, "Just talk, just keep talking." So she said, "I've made this commitment to my family and I'm committed to our work as a spiritual group, as well." It was like the sky opened a little bit and I said, "Just keep saying more things," and she did. She said things that somehow made me know that I wasn't going to need to give up my spiritual commitment if I left . . . that there were many ways to free your soul . . . one could live a family life and that her caring for her children was part of her commitment to God and her commitment to her husband was part of that, too . . . and I would say, "I hope I'll be able to help people," and she said, "Clara, you already are . . . you already have helped many people," . . . things like that . . . It was very, very important. And I hung up the phone and then I called her back ten minutes later and said, "Say some more things," and the crack got a little bigger.

Clara stayed up all night. Over and over, she played a tape of Mother Theresa talking about working with the poor, about kindness and Christ.

It was sort of lovely to be close to that . . . to get some perspective. I could feel my response . . . wanting to heal and wanting to help. She was expressing my resonance with that, particularly the kindness . . . the kindness was all gone from the group by that time . . . just the gentle kindness I could feel, that I have and that somehow I had betrayed a lot during that time. So I listened to that tape . . . and then at one point I realized that the energy that I thought we were working with was in *me*, and that it would be in me even if I left the group . . . I really had that experience, it was not just mental but all the way through me. When I realized that, I knew I could leave. I decided that was what I needed to do. I wrote a note: "I'm leaving the group. It is no longer a place that I want to be. I don't know what my service will be but I know that it needs to involve family and children more than this does." The next morning I dropped it in Alex's box and then I ran into Hugh almost immediately afterwards.

Leaving was not joyful. Clara had joined Life Force because it made her feel loved and accepted, and it had been a way to help others. At this point she felt worthless, evil, and alone, and she doubted her ability to help anyone.

For a week I didn't tell anyone that I had left except Hugh. I just sat upstairs in a chair . . . The first night I kept feeling that there was an enormous cloud of darkness just off my finger-tips or on the edge of the room or certainly down in the direc-tion of the Center. I had to keep it out, I had to protect myself from it . . . I made a circle on the floor of a book of Gandhi and the Mother Theresa tape and I had a picture by Kathe Kollwitz of Mary and Elizabeth embracing . . . like a protec-tive circle, good friends who had made a spiritual commit-ment to the world. I wanted them near me. The great fear was that I was bad. The picture of my future was that I would do penance . . . redeem myself in some way. I volunteered at a nearby hospital on the cancer ward and I worked there three mornings a week for the next few months. I just wanted to give people water and hold their hand . . . I was still grappling with maybe I was really bad . . . I wrote and wrote and wrote about it in my journal. I kept wishing someone would tell me that I was good and I also knew that that wouldn't do it. Even-tually [in meditation] I was saying to something deep in my-self, "I really do want to help," and I heard a voice say, "I know you do." And then it was all right . . . that was the turning point . . . then I knew that I was still good, that I was still the person who wanted to love and wanted to make my commit-ment to love. I didn't really wonder about it after that time. Working it through on my own was real important . . . some-thing I had to figure out for myself that I don't think anyone else could have told me. I feel proud of that moment . . . of staying with that.

Clara had hoped that when she left the group, Hugh would also. But he did not, although he knew that as long as he stayed he would not see his child, since contact was not allowed between those in the group and those who had left.

HUGH: For some reason, I'd made a vow to stay a year, no matter what happened. I was going to go on and do great spiritual work.

Hugh was expected to have no contact with Clara, to give her no money, no support, just to wipe the slate clean. He was told that Clara had left the group because she had become identified with her evil part, that all the good qualities she had were left in the group.

HUGH: Luckily we had this wonderful friend . . . I wasn't about to abandon Clara so I sent money through her. There was contact with this woman friend from both of us. I would go there for dinner and we would talk a little bit about Clara and I would say, "Is Clara angry at me?" And she said, "Oh, Hugh, Clara loves you so much!" She would say the same thing to Clara . . . So, slowly, over those months there was an indirect healing or reconnection.

After several months Clara sent a letter to Hugh through their mutual friend, secretly, apologizing for what had happened and sharing her distress over the events. Hugh phoned Clara and over the next few weeks they had several clandestine contacts.

HUGH: There was the beginning of trust and love flowing again between us . . . and Clara asking me some wonderful questions . . . Not pushing me but saying, What do you see? Is this the kind of group that Christ would be near? Is this really the way people who love each other treat one another?

Hugh also contacted others who had left the group, setting up clandestine meetings at street corners or in cars.

Having gained in confidence from these contacts, Hugh then wrote to the executive committee stating that he needed to make an arrangement to take care of his son, to spend time with him, and that he also needed time for his music. Hugh was immediately put back into quarantine.

HUGH: It was the sixth or seventh time it happened—this was the first time I wasn't paralyzed with fear. I started cataloging my fears . . . I would sit there in quarantine in my room and write down all the different levels of fear I had. It was fascinating . . . fear of inadequacy, fear of damnation, fear of becoming just a vegetable. They were still giving me tapes of the meetings and I would listen to the tapes and I'd draw a line down the middle of the page and I'd write down on one side the world view that was being put out in the group that I could buy, and then I would write down on the other side what I could see actually happening . . . It was fascinating because the things that Alex was describing, what these subjective [evil] entities were supposedly doing "out there" to us were precisely the things that he was doing in relationship to the group, right there. You could hear it on the tapes. I was holding these two world views side by side. That was where I felt the most schizophrenic, the most stressed . . . I had this image of the back of an envelope with "I quit" on it, and I knew that if I began to crack that I would grab the nearest piece of paper, write "I quit" on it, stick it in Alex's mailbox and run out the door. But I wanted to find out as much as I could about what was going on before I left.

During the last year of Hugh's involvement, the group and Alex Monroe had deteriorated markedly. Paranoia pervaded the members' lives. Fantasies had acquired so much power that even sensate perception changed to accommodate the group's delusional world. Alex's focus on past lives had become more pervasive. His fantasies included a particularly malignant creature who was cruel, cunning, scheming, manipulative, and very smart, very beautiful, and an assortment of other characters, including devils with wings—a complete cosmos.

HUGH: People would begin to see them [the devils], and then call teams to protect them. We had all become very paranoid by then . . . I would spend hours . . . fourteen or fifteen hours in a row on the phone, protecting [group members] and fighting some subjective entity who was attacking somebody else. Barbara Monroe was one who seemed to be attacked a lot . . . she would call and say this particular entity, "Charlie," a big, black devil with wings, was attacking her . . . we would call in the forces of light and we would do a visualization. To fight the dark force you would bring in an angel of light, an archangel with a sword . . . light against dark in imagery. Barbara would get better, or she would get over her migraine headache or whatever . . . Each person had their kind of private devils. It would happen among the Executive Committee and then we'd hear about it and have to clean it up. Each of the Executive Committee had his or her own [devil]. One had a panther-like cat, another this disembodied head and another this dark archangel, and so forth.

Such so-called subjective work had come to occupy more and more of the group's time, particularly as a team of three or four members would be giving support to meetings or processing sessions by conducting a group visualization of their own. Subjective work was extended to cover phone calls, not only within the group, but to people outside the group as well. The members could not go to sleep until protective measures were taken for members of the inner circle and for anyone designated as having trouble.

CLARA: At the end of a day's work, there would be a team that would call you and say, "Before you go to bed tonight, would you 'clean up' Erica? Would you 'clean up' Debbie? 'Clean up' their clothes and shop and stuff?" There would be this protection we would put around the whole group before we could go to sleep and that would take forever . . . we'd be falling asleep.

HUGH: By the end of my time [in the group] we were doing it [subjective work] almost exclusively, fourteen, fifteen, sixteen hours a day. The Executive Committee was so paranoid and Alex was so paranoid he stayed in his room the whole time and everyone else was in apartments and the Executive Committee couldn't even meet in the same room together for fear that they would do numbers on each other, trips, power trips, seduction trips, so forth . . . There were always teams "cleaning up" the Executive Committee so the Executive Committee could meet. Alex, also, was having to work with all four of them, there were only four Executives left by then [all women] . . . the men were gone . . . Alex and his women were all that was left.

HUGH: I knew I was going to leave . . . the more I talked to Clara, the clearer that became. I waited ten days and then a phone call came in the afternoon . . . it was Alex and another Executive, supposedly to talk about my letter. So they started in . . . I was able to stand up to Alex for about an hour. I told him, "I'm in touch with my soul but I see the group over here in a corner, I'm no longer connected to the group." He was furious . . . he attacked . . . I stood up to it for a while and then I just went [under] . . . as we all did . . . The best you

could do was pretend . . . just try and bear it and hope it
would be over soon.

The processing proceeded—all by telephone. Alex portrayed
Clara and Hugh's son, David, as interpenetrated by a devil. It was
done through suggestions:

ALEX: Are you thinking of going back to Clara?

HUGH: Well, that would depend but I certainly want to have
some contact with her around David.

ALEX: Close your eyes and see Clara.

Alex would then evoke from Hugh's memory all the negative
things that Clara had done to him.

ALEX: How do you feel about that, Hugh?

HUGH: I feel angry.

Then Hugh was sent to the special catharsis room at the Center where he ventilated his anger at Clara for two hours.

HUGH: I knew there were two things going on. I was play
acting it to some degree because I knew this was the kind of
thing I would go through and on the other hand, it was so
powerful, it was real. And it did reinforce once again, the negative image of Clara. It was a kind of shared fantasy of paranoia in which Alex's view of how things were would be infil-
trated into the person's head through strong emotional
reinforcement because he could get this anger out . . . That
night I got out a lot of rage at Clara which I am sure was connected with the fact that I felt she had betrayed me. Then he
would feed the feeling of betrayal and anger with images and
slanted questions, "Who do you see behind Clara?" knowing
full well and my knowing full well that it was supposed to be
one of Alex's imaginary characters. "And what's she doing?"
And then, "What do they [Clara and David] want to do to
your heart? They don't want to love it do they?" It was that
kind of leading question. He'd never say, "They want to eat
your heart, Hugh," he'd get you to say it and then he'd reinforce it. "Yes, yes, they want to eat your heart and it's wrong,
Hugh; it's a sin. It's wrong to love them." Alex implied that
Clara and David just wanted my money and were loving me

in order to get my money and not for myself. "They don't deserve your love. They can't use your love. The people who need your love are the students in the training program." It was that kind of thing.

Alex would give [you] a choice, he would say, "Well, you don't want to live your life that way [selfishly], do you?" And you'd say, "No, no, I know I don't." "Well then, . . ." It was a kind of nod to psychological processing in terms of catharsis, making choices, intention, higher values, but it became increasingly Alex projecting whatever was in his mind into people.

The processing continued for eight hours. Although Hugh tried to fake compliance he was terrified of the strong images that had been summoned. He could not prevent Alex from affecting him.

I don't understand this, but this happened for other people, too, at the end of these eight hours there was this experience of love for Alex, and his love for me, and a kind of intimacy that was very compelling. I apologized to him for making it hard for him, that he'd had to spend these eight hours with me . . . and then he wept on the phone and I wept, and he said, "Oh, that helps so much," and I said how much I loved him.

I woke up the next morning and it was like I couldn't find my head. Everything that I had put together had been shattered. I had been really beat up . . . I had been under severe attack from people who thought they were saving me from the devil. Looking back it feels like a snake whispering in my ears for eight hours. This ear is still slightly deaf . . . the hearing has never totally come back on this side.

However, Hugh was prepared. He went back to the notes he had taken so carefully and reconstructed what had happened. The battle to leave was a struggle against intense fear.

The point of highest tension for me was to figure out what reality system did I want to commit to. Alex was saying, "You need to turn away from your child and Clara and never even *think* about them anymore. There should be no contact. Nothing. Just turn away." I was so afraid . . . fear of damnation is what it finally became and Alex would reinforce it . . . images of outer darkness, gnashing of teeth, just total and utter damnation . . . I had to go against that, I had to pit against that the principle that a father does not leave his child. I couldn't believe that God wanted me to leave my child for anything. I said, "Even if I'm damned forever, even if I'm going to be cast into outer darkness, I'm not going to turn against David." That saved me, woke me up. I'm so glad, I'm so grateful.

Despite this resolve, there were times during that last week when the pull of Alex and the group would threaten to overwhelm him. At one point Hugh phoned Clara in a panic.

I could feel a maelstrom, a vortex and I was going to lose my will and be sucked into the center of this thing . . . I could see in the center . . . this nice, cozy place, where all your needs were taken care of and it was loving. I remember writing down in big letters, "I've got to get out of here!"

In the last few weeks before leaving Life Force, Hugh was helped by talking with another group member, Jerry (although communication between them had been forbidden), about his perceptions of what Alex was doing.

At last there was contact with someone inside the group who saw things the way I did. There was just an explosion of talk . . . clandestine . . . after the work was over we'd call each other up and talk.

Finally, a week after the processing session, Hugh wrote a letter of resignation. The next morning, very early, he placed a copy on each member's doorstep and then left the city.

The word went out that I was the anti-Christ and that my resignation letter was to be picked up with tongs, put in another envelope, sealed and burned. Everything I'd ever given to anybody—loaned a bed or a book or whatever—were to be destroyed or turned in. The interesting thing was that the people who were there were feeling closer and closer to the Christ while all this was going on.

Hugh stayed in communication with Jerry, helping him to leave also.

HUGH: [Jerry would say,] "I'm sitting here and my whole body is shaking and trembling with fear . . . it's rising off the bed . . . my heart is shaking . . . if I bought the system, I would say that you were the devil and you were seducing me away from the group."

And I would say, "O.K., what's true?" I'd just sit there. "What's true?" And then he would gradually [say,] "I know that's not true . . ." We spent a long time on the phone where he would go through the same process that I'd gone through. It was just like a buffer zone of terror around the group that a person had to cross. It was almost necessary to have a person on the outside.

Jerry left the organization soon after. Hugh's leaving set off a chain of resignations; each person who departed helped others to leave. A packet of letters of resignation was circulated among the graduate students, most of whom then left. With so many of the staff gone, the graduate school closed. Shortly thereafter, Alex Monroe and the remaining group members went underground, moving to another city where they were said to be spending their entire time processing each other.

■　　■　　■

The story of Hugh and Clara Robinson illustrates what can happen when thought and perception come to be controlled by desire and fear. The psychological damage the Robinsons suffered in the cult process was extensive; their sense of self-worth, emotional stability, and relationships with those closest to them were badly battered. Indeed, many months after leaving the group, the Robinsons were still recovering from the trauma of the experience.

Readers may wonder how different Hugh and Clara were from themselves. After all, prior to joining Life Force, Clara had become very anxious; Hugh was discontented, uncomfortable with his life. Yet, to us in the seminar, the Robinsons did not seem very different from most people. After further interviews (which I conducted myself), I found no reason to change that assessment.

Although the world of Life Force may seem alien to most of us, in a number of important ways Hugh and Clara's experience was not qualitatively different from that which occurs in everyday society, although it was more radical, more intense, less subject to moderating influences and, consequently, more pathological.

Analysis of Hugh and Clara's experience and that of others involved with cults reveals four basic behaviors found in extreme form in cults: compliance with the group, dependence on a leader, devaluing the outsider, and avoiding dissent. These behaviors are not distinct and independent but interrelated. In my view, they arise in part from what I refer to as the dependency dream, the regressive wish for security that uses the family as a model, creating an authoritarian leadership structure (the parent) and a close-knit, exclusive group (the children). Since the leader-parent has many of the insecurities of the follower-child, reality must be distorted by both to maintain the child's illusion (or wish) that the parent can always provide protection, that he or she has no weaknesses. Dissent is stifled because it casts doubt on the perfection of the leader and the special status of the group. Group compliance preserves security by supporting the beliefs crucial to the fantasy of superiority, beliefs which also explain the powers and entitlement of the leader and can no more be challenged than he or she. Outsiders, non-believers, are excluded and devalued for they do not believe what the group believes; if the group and leader are superior, the outsider is inferior.

Because group boundaries are more permeable in everyday society, hidden ("normal") cult behavior is not as intense as in overt cults, and the relative importance of one or the other of these interlocking behaviors may vary considerably depending on the social organization being studied.

In the next chapters, I will describe how cult behaviors are manifested in everyday life in our society, using examples from large corporations, religion, psychiatry, the media, and government. I do not mean to imply that other levels of motivation are not active also, but they are conscious. The danger of the longing for the back seat of the car—is that because it is usually unconscious, it can powerfully influence us in ways that are not recognized.

We recognize an overt threat from powerful authorities, be it loss of job, injury to self or loved ones, or imprisonment. Likewise, most people are very aware of the lure of money, fame, and power. However, we are not accustomed to recognizing the effect on us of the threats and rewards of childhood's world: the parental frown or the parental smile, the invitation to play or the exclusion from a game, the blissful comfort of being cared for.

The dependency dream acts as an unseen regressive force, shaping our behavior to accomplish the desires of childhood while we are pursuing the goals of adults. It produces unconscious submission to the beliefs and demands of authorities. It leads us to seek reassurance by repeating dogma, to attack outsiders, to ignore and devalue dissenting opinions. Unwillingness to disrupt the fantasy that we have a wise, strong parent in charge leads us to accept the limits of debate established by authorities and the beliefs upon which those authorities depend. Thus, the anxiety evoked by a cult situation is not often recognized for what it is. Even when fear of the leader is conscious, a person is not usually aware that it may be based on the persistence in adulthood of a child's desire and vulnerability, as much as on any realistic need or possibility of reprisal.

Although a deprived or traumatic childhood may result in greater vulnerability to cult manipulation or deceit, the experience of childhood itself renders us susceptible to the blissful promise of a safe, secure way to return home. A continuum of behavior exists, from the People's Temple to Life Force, to rigid religious groups, corporate cultures, professional societies, and ordinary us/them categories.

What I wish to stress is not that every group is a cult, but that cult thinking is the effect of psychological forces endemic to the human mind, and that these forces operate in the everyday life of each of us; they distort perception, bias thinking, and inculcate belief. Our own behavior brings us closer to the experience of Hugh and Clara than we would like to believe.

Compliance with the Group

HUMAN beings are social beings. Mother, father, siblings, grandparents, and other relatives form our first social group. The family into which we are born has enormous influence upon us, not only because a long and complex learning process takes place before adulthood and self-sufficiency are attained, but also because the family becomes the paradigm for other social groups. In fact, most social groups share characteristics of family groups with members who occupy dominant (parent) and subordinate (child) roles. By considering the characteristics that social groups share with families, we can understand why individuals who are considered independent and adult outside the group may become dependent and childlike within it.

Of course, the family's adults—who transmit social attitudes, fears, and hopes to the child—are themselves subject to the influence of larger social units toward which they may have many of the same dependency feelings that their child has toward them. These overlapping *reference groups* are composed of friends, colleagues, and/or people of similar religious and political persuasions. Reference groups influence our behavior greatly, although we may not be conscious of how and when this occurs.

Conformity to characteristic views, dress, and conduct differentiate social groupings, marking the most outwardly rebellious as well as the most conventional.[1] An amusing example comes from my own field of psychiatry. Janet Malcolm relates the experience of an analyst of the New York Psychoanalytic Institute who, shortly after he graduated, purchased a black and white herringbone tweed jacket which enormously pleased him. Two years later he met a fellow analyst wearing an almost identical jacket. "My colleague laughed and said, 'But, you know, everyone at the New York Psychoanalytic wears this kind of jacket.' So then I understood why I had felt so great about my jacket. I began to look around the Institute and, sure enough, the jacket was all over the place."[2]

Imitation of our peers is basic to learning and development and the reference group is an important influence throughout life. Social psychologist Albert Bandura and his colleagues were able to cure children of nursery school age of fear of dogs by the simple procedure of having them watch another child playing happily with a dog. Even when films were used instead of actual demonstrations, the procedure worked. Even more striking was the research of psychologist Robert O'Connor on socially withdrawn school children who typically stayed on the fringes of peer group activities. Believing that their behavior predicted a pattern of lifelong isolation and social unease, and trying to change that pattern, O'Connor put together a film composed of eleven different nursery school scenes. Each scene showed a different solitary child observing a social activity and then joining in, to everyone's pleasure. O'Connor tried the film on a group of the most severely withdrawn children from four nursery schools. The results were impressive.

> After watching the film, the isolates immediately began to interact with their peers at a level equal to that of the normal children in the schools. Even more astonishing was that O'Connor found when he returned to the schools six weeks later to observe. While the withdrawn children who had not seen O'Connor's film remained as isolated as ever, those who *had* viewed it were now leading their schools in amount of social activity. It seems that this 23-minute movie, viewed just once, was enough to reverse a potential pattern of lifelong maladaptive behavior.[3]

Yet, as we know, the power of group influence has its negative side and not only in cults. For example, research indicates that the reason a group of bystanders may not come to the aid of a victim is not that they are indifferent, heartless or "numbed by urban living," but because in uncertain situations each person looks to others for cues as to how to interpret and react to what is happening. Each person's passivity reinforces that of others. In contrast, when researchers enacted an "emergency" in the presence of a single bystander, that person invariably responded helpfully, whether in a city or not. Clearly, reliance on social cues, not empathy, is the issue.

Robert Cialdini, an experimental social psychologist, explains the group's influence on our behavior as being utilitarian.

> The tendency to see an action as more appropriate when others are doing it works quite well normally. As a rule, we will make fewer mistakes by acting in accord with social evidence than contrary to it. Usually, when a lot of people are doing something, it is the right thing to do.[4]

But every society provides numerous examples of group influence which turned out to be injurious to the group itself, as well as unfair and harmful to others. How and why do groups affect their members so strongly?

■　■　■

The remarkable influence of groups upon their members has been of interest to psychologists and psychiatrists for a long time. Gustave Le Bon was one of the first to study the behavior of people in crowds and mobs. Writing in 1895 about such situations, he described "the disappearance of the conscious personality, the predominance of the unconscious personality, the turning by means of suggestion and contagion of feelings and ideas in an identical direction, the tendency to immediately transform the suggested ideas into acts."[5]

Freud believed that these characteristics could be explained as a regression to a primitive mental activity, that of the primal horde. "The primitive form of human society was that of a horde ruled over despotically by a powerful male . . . Just as primitive man survives potentially in every individual, so the primal horde may arise once more out of any random collection."[6]

Freud went on to emphasize

the contrivance by means of which an artificial group is held
together and the constitution of the primal horde. We have
seen that with an army and a Church this contrivance is the
illusion that the leader loves all of the individuals equally and
justly. But this is simply an idealistic remodelling of the state
of affairs in the primal horde, where all of the sons knew that
they were equally *persecuted* by the primal father, and *feared*
him equally.[7]

Freud's analysis—its exclusively male focus aside—would
seem to have applicability in the case of the Life Force group,
where the initial feeling of the members of being loved by Alex
gave way to fear of him.

Since Freud, the theory of group psychology has been expanded. British psychoanalyst Wilfred Bion, drawing on Melanie
Klein's ideas about primitive psychological defenses in the infant
and young child, studied small-group phenomena and concluded
that groups tend to adopt, unconsciously, one of three primitive
emotional states—dependency, pairing, or fight-flight. Bion called
these states basic assumptions, and thought of them as expressive
of disowned impulses. He saw any group as likely to exhibit irrational behavior, indicating that one of the three assumptions is
operating. What Bion designates as the dependency-assumption
group is a very good description of the state of mind prevailing in
cults.

The essential aim [of the dependency-assumption group] . . .
is to attain security through and have its members protected
by one individual. It assumes that this is why the group has
met. The members act as if they know nothing, as if they are
inadequate and immature creatures. Their behavior implies
that the leader, by contrast, is omnipotent and omniscient.[8]

Object relations theorist D. W. Winnicott has suggested that
the group may represent a transitional object for its members,
who express regressive themes appropriate to that stage of development. Going further, Jungian analyst Arthur Colman, drawing
on the work of Margaret Mahler, has proposed that group consciousness is a developmental phase prior to full individuation.[9]

All these theorists endeavor to explain the powerful effect of groups from the point of view of the psychology of the individuals that compose them. However, from a sociobiological point of view, there is another basis for understanding why the group should be so influential: human survival has been enhanced by the tendency for families to combine in bands or tribes for mutual protection and support. As banishment from the larger group could endanger an individual's survival, an acute sensitivity to the group's wishes and requirements probably carried an evolutionary advantage. Socially aware, adept individuals would eventually dominate the genetic pool through the process of natural selection. Perhaps in this way the human race has developed a high awareness of the wishes, fears, and requirements of the groups on which each person depends. Such an evolutionary process may explain why certain basic group reactions and fantasies (such as those described by Bion) seem to take place regardless of the member's actual family experience.

Certainly, whatever theoretical model or models one might prefer, the desire for group approval and the fear of disapproval remain with us as very powerful controlling forces. In the Robinsons' case, Hugh's testimony makes clear how much his need for the group's approval influenced him, especially when he was in quarantine, and Clara recalled how seductive it was for the group to praise her while criticizing Hugh. Furthermore, numerous experiments show how a group can change the perceptions of its members, can even foster and maintain a bizarre, paranoid worldview such as that which developed within the Life Force executive group.

We can feel secure in the protection provided by a group but that protection has its price. Compliance with the group often extends further than acceptance of the group's views to include participation in the attack on deviants by subtle (or not so subtle) disapproval, punishment, or rejection of any member who voices criticism of the consensus or disagrees with the leader. Dissident is criticized as disloyal, lacking commitment, interfering with the important work of the group.

As a psychotherapist, I frequently work with people oppressed by a punitive, controlling internal figure who lashes them with guilt and mocks with disapproval. Exploring the reason for this oppression, we often find that its purpose is to insure conformity to the group upon whose approval they depend and whose rejection they fear.

Although most social groups encourage dependency and compliance in civilized ways, the basic pattern can usually be discerned.

■   ■   ■

Pressures encouraging dependency, present in most groups, are intensified in a cult. As we saw in the case of Hugh and Clara, extreme dependence on the cult is fostered by isolating the member from other sources of self-esteem, financial support, and emotional closeness. Consequently, the cult's ability to reward or punish is markedly enhanced. With this in mind it is not surprising that a particularly pernicious feature of cults—and often an index of their power over their members—is the attack on couples and families. In the case of Life Force, not a single couple who began with the group survived intact, even the marriage of Alex and Barbara Monroe failed. This destructive effect is characteristic of the stronger cults; the power of the leader and the sense of security of the group are diminished by any strong social bonds which set up conflicting loyalties. (Hugh and Clara's enduring bonds to their child and to each other eventually provided the motivation to break from the group.) Thus, powerful cult groups often attack the couple through arranged marriages, the breaking of love relationships by order of the leader or the group, pressure toward group marriage or chastity, sexual relationships with the leader, and/or interfere with the bonds between parents and children.

In her study of communes and utopian communities, sociologist Rosabeth Kanter described how in the previous century such groups coped with the threat to cohesiveness posed by two-person intimacy.

> Successful nineteenth century groups often discouraged couples in one of two extreme and experientially opposite ways—either through free love, including group marriage, in which every member was expected to have intimate sexual relations with all others, or through celibacy, in which no member could have sexual relations with any other.[10]

She cites the Oneida community, which had been notorious for its practice of free love.

Every member had sexual access to every other with his or her consent, while fidelity was negatively sanctioned; preference of one member for another was quickly discouraged. When two members of the community showed a marked preference of one member for one another, they were asked to mate with two others.[11]

In such communities, ties between parents and children were minimized by varying degrees of communal childcare and by restricted contact between mother and child. In the Life Force group this was accomplished by making inordinate demands on Clara's time and devaluing her contribution as a mother, even labelling it selfish.

The weakening of family structures is not only an issue of loyalty. The role of parent and the roles of husband and wife are adult roles, whereas in a cult the leader and the group together constitute a parent-child structure in which adult autonomy has no place. For this reason it is in the cult's interest to foster the regression of its members to a pre-adult phase of psychosexual development, and such a regression is usually easy to observe. A family unit resists this push.

The attack on couples and families is usually restricted to tightly controlled groups that set themselves off from the surrounding society. Seldom is it a significant factor in ordinary society. However, the weakening of ties to others so as to strengthen dependency on the group and leader can be observed in strongly authoritarian political systems such as that which prevailed in Germany's Third Reich. The Hitler Youth were encouraged to regard parents as potential enemies of the glorious new Germany, to inform on them and to turn them in to the Gestapo for comments critical of the Nazi regime. Many did so. Parents came to fear and distrust their children, while the children scorned their parents as being weak, obstructionist or traitors.[12] Mao Tse-tung encouraged a similar split between the generations of China.

.   .   .

Compliance and dependency can be strongly enhanced by the group's eliciting a powerful emotional experience. Lowell Streiker, a researcher who interviewed converts to revivalism, gives a composite description of a conversion experience as it typically occurs in a small revivalist group or church.

> The prospect is directly confronted with his sins. His physical and psychic space are invaded by these self-confident strangers. He is discomforted and thrown off balance. He becomes anxious. The group tells him that his feelings are caused by his sinfulness. He is overcome with guilt and sadness. He realizes that his life is not working. Eagerly he confesses his shortcomings—sexual lapses, lies, petty thievery, drug abuse, and so forth. Guided by the group, he prays that God will forgive him and receive him as His child. He is urged, "Ask Jesus to come into your heart." He does, and the inner turmoil subsides. The recruit senses an inner release and relief. The hugs and congratulations of the group tell him that he belongs, that he has identity, that he is accepted. Many ecstatic converts report, "It was as though a great weight had been lifted from my shoulders."[13]

Streiker suggests that such groups create an unbearable tension in the person on whom they are focusing, and that the sudden release from that tension—"accepting the Lord into your heart" or "surrender to Jesus"—is interpreted as a spiritual experience, being "born again." He goes on to comment, "When Jesus told Nicodemus of the need to be "born again" he did not badger his hearer until he underwent a group-coerced, programmed, stereotyped purgation."[14]

Of course, to be born again does not require a specifically Christian context. Listen again to Clara Robinson:

> So I went up towards the sun and there was this wise man and he said to me, "My child", and I climbed in his lap, like a child—he was very much like a father—as I retell it I realize that . . . I just felt like I was home . . . I felt a downflow of love and affection that I have never felt before or since. . . . It was that experience that made me feel that I needed to do more of whatever this system was.

Groups may enhance compliance and dependency by producing a variety of altered states of consciousness that are easily misinterpreted to conform with the beliefs and interests of the group. Hugh and Clara Robinson always had an intuitive sense of a larger reality that was very important to them. That perception was confused with unresolved dependency longings, leading them to interpret the initial guided daydream as being spiritual and to accept the Monroes as guides or agents in that domain. A variety of techniques—chanting, singing, dancing, sleep deprivation, meditation—can produce a state of consciousness quite impressive to the participant. The event may then be offered as proof of the group's value or the leader's spiritual power—the convert's wish to believe does the rest.

Demonstrations of psychic ability are especially potent in this respect, and Yogic disciplines, in particular, seem to have a technology for producing phenomena unexplainable by current scientific knowledge. Some years ago, while investigating a popular Eastern cult, I underwent an initiation in which a Yogi placed his hand on my head and I then experienced a spot of intense white light blazing briefly in the center of my mind—or so it seemed. This was interpreted (by the cult) as contact with the divine and proof that the guru was a new messiah. I still don't understand how the man did it, but the spot of light was just that—a spot of light—and no more a demonstration of the divine than turning on the faucet would be to someone who knows nothing about plumbing. Indeed, the mystical literature warns repeatedly that such experiences are distractions and should be ignored.[15] (Nevertheless, this particular group's converts eagerly practiced the prescribed meditations hoping to repeat the experience and rushed to take part in any further initiations that were made available to them.)

Unfortunately, legitimate but subtle intimations of the spiritual that may have led a convert to search for a group and teacher may be displaced by such dramatic alterations of consciousness, which can then become a further basis for control. Just as the group's emotional support and validation can be provided or withdrawn, so can the dramatic pseudo-spiritual experiences. Before long, the positive force of idealism and service that may have been foremost in a convert's mind when joining a cult becomes corrupted by fear

of deprivation and abandonment. As we saw in Life Force, idealistic concepts are then subverted when they are used to rationalize
behavior a convert would have condemned before joining the
group.

．　　．　　．

A major way a group exerts power is through threat of censure
and expulsion, classifying the deviant as bad. I had occasion to
learn about this firsthand a few years ago when I became involved
in the anti-nuclear movement. (At that time I would not have believed that liberals such as myself could behave like cult members,
although I was certain that right-wingers did.) The story is worth
telling because it may connect with the reader's own prejudices
and provide an experience of the very dynamic I am discussing.

In 1980 I attended a weekend conference given by Physicians
for Social Responsibility, entitled "The Medical Consequences of
Nuclear Weapons and Nuclear War." The presentations were intended to impress the audience with the ghastly consequences of
nuclear war. That goal was certainly achieved; we were left in a
state of great alarm and dread. I responded by becoming active in
spreading the word about the enormous danger and the immediate steps that should be taken. (This was not a new role for me; I
had been active in the 1960s in the effort to stop the atmospheric
testing of nuclear weapons. Now the menace was worse and the
catastrophic aspects more overwhelming.) I raised questions with
other PSR members about what action people might take to increase their chances of survival if a nuclear war did occur. I was
told that there was nothing that could be done; shelters were described as useless and prevention of nuclear war as the only answer. Some speakers declared that anyone who undertook civil
defense planning was immoral, engaged in "a highly unethical act."

These summary judgments were not convincing to me, and I
began reading outside the peace movement literature, encountering other points of view and other facts. Eventually, I came to the
judgment that regional food stockpiles would save millions of
lives if a war did occur and that establishing such stockpiles would

not accelerate the arms race or give people a false sense of security, but would be a logical and appropriate response to a very real danger. Furthermore, I believed that people should be told the less alarming facts about radiation danger and about what protection a shelter could and could not offer.

When I mentioned these ideas to my friends in the peace movement, they would draw back slightly, their eyes would narrow, and I could see them mentally remove my name from the file of "good guys" and transfer it to the one marked "bad guys." (Perhaps you, the reader, have been having a similar reaction.)

I promoted a lecture about protection against a variety of radiation hazards including nuclear explosions. Almost no one came, except some protesters from the peace movement. With the radiologist who gave the lecture, I later appeared on a radio talk show. It was clear the host found it hard to grasp that although I was in favor of stockpiling food, a civil defense measure, I was opposed to the MX missiles and favored a nuclear freeze. He had assumed, as did others, that I must be a hawk. A cult-like propensity for a black-and-white division of the world was all too obvious.

This publicity, along with an interview published in a local newspaper, generated a response whose character and vehemence caught me by surprise. I was roundly attacked. No one from the peace movement asked me *why* I thought what I did. They weren't curious at all; they had simply decided I had become a hardliner, an immoral survivalist. The arguments advanced against my views seemed simplistic and illogical, much like the recitations of dogma I was familiar with from my study of religious cults.

In addition to seeing cult processes at work in others, I became aware that I was influenced by them. I began to avoid mentioning my views to acquaintances and even some friends, for fear of being cast out. Educational as the experience proved, being regarded as a bad guy within my own group was quite unpleasant. At one public hearing where I testified, I was attacked by a peace movement contingent who used the same rhetoric that I had used in the past as part of that same group. It was startling to be on the receiving end, to be the object of the glaring hostile eyes and the impassioned appeals to humanity. Ruefully, I realized that in the past I had been similarly self-indulgent in obtaining the emotional satisfaction that springs from being righteous in a good cause. I would not have known that I was to some degree a member of a cult had I not challenged my group's dogma.

．　　■　　■

Compliance with a group increases with one's psychological and economic dependence on it. This can be seen in many social institutions, including the corporations that dominate modern economic life.

Sociologist Diane Margolis studied the managers at a large corporation and found that the one effect of frequent transfers was to decrease a husband and wife's involvement in local politics and community life and to increase their dependence on the friends and activities of their particular corporate world. Moreover, they learned to buy their homes with a view to resale and this tended to place them in housing areas occupied by other corporation managers. Economic and social segregation played an important role in the corporation's becoming, for many managers, the chief source of self-esteem, companionship, and personal expression. For the managers of many corporations

> needs usually fulfilled by human relationships become increasingly difficult to satisfy because almost all relationships outside their nuclear families are distant and fleeting. So like half-starved people who in the absence of proteins will fatten but not nourish themselves on starches, managers and their families hunger for goods money cannot buy, but reach for those it can. Each year salary increases put these within easier reach, and the manager's family finds that every purchase just whets the appetite for the next. . . . He knew he was in a game he could never win, but he played on. For him it was the only game in town.[16]

To leave the company would mean all that sacrifice has been in vain; security must be given up. Wishful thinking tends to replace critical assessment just as it did with the Robinsons who also had to face giving up a "warm cocoon." With few connections to the outside world that world can easily appear less desirable—and the corporation more valuable—than it is.

.   .   .

Although corporations do not attack the family directly in the manner of cults such as Life Force, most of them do require the subordination of the manager's family's needs to those of the corporation. This sacrifice is demanded as the price of career advancement.

A common practice is to promote managers by transferring them every year or two to positions in other parts of the country. Then their positions are filled by others who are moved in; a game of musical chairs takes place.

Certainly, it is in the corporation's interest to give managers wide experience and also to test their commitment to the company; however, the interests of the manager's children are served poorly. (Although corporations have begun paying more attention to this problem, the transfer is still a standard feature of corporate life.) Indeed, in my psychotherapy practice I often encounter people who have been socially impaired by frequent family moves that made them perpetually new kids on the block; just when friendships were established, their families would move again. Such children learn to limit their friendships to avoid the pain of loss and tend to interpret other children's reserve toward them when they arrive in a new town as indicating that they are not likable. For many wives the process is almost as painful.

> If people know you're going to move, they start to disengage themselves from you, too . . . you find them backing off . . . You start finding out that they're not there anymore. They're busy. And they're busy with things they know they're going to be doing after you've left. You notice it. . . . people starting to draw back. And the kids, I know, would say they couldn't get any friends to come and play. The other kids would suddenly be busy with somebody else, even though they've al-

ways been with them. Their friends were starting to find somebody else because after all, "she's leaving."[17]

Frequent transfers are also ruinous to a spouse's career ambitions. The wife of a Schlumberger manager stationed in Cairo summed it up:

Sometimes you really feel lost . . . The man has a job to do. You have nothing to do. So you have babies to keep you busy. Or you join a club. If you say, "I want to have a career of my own," and say you don't want to go where your husband goes, then you're headed for the divorce courts.[18]

Commitment to the corporation is also measured by a manager's willingness to take work home at night and on weekends and to be absent from his family on frequent business trips. In the competition for a manager's time, energy, and attention the corporation is out to win. Conflicts that arise between family needs and corporate needs—which may have the look of accidental occurrences—are sometimes deliberate tests of the person's commitment, the outcomes of which are carefully noted. The manager who chooses family over the corporation fails the test, as does the family.

Furthermore, wives may become unpaid company employees as they fall in line to support the careers of their husbands.

They [the managers] are . . . corporate men, not family men. Wives must actively subordinate themselves to the husbands' work aims or, at the very least, not interfere with them. The key to an effective partnership . . . (would be) the degree to which the wife actively adopted the corporate goals and skillfully aided the husband in that direction. This makes the wife a kind of high-class assistant bound by marriage rather than salary but otherwise facilitating the work goals with the same sense of efficiency the husband would expect of his secretary and other office personnel. The all-embracing demands of corporate life do not permit distraction.[19]

Within the corporate culture of many companies, it is assumed that the corporate goals and the husband's career should have first priority in much the same way that Life Force and other cults regard their own activities as primary and the competing demands of marriage and family as distinctly secondary. As Harold Geneen, former chief executive officer of ITT put it: "The first requirement of a senior executive is instant availability. He must put his firm above his family; he must be prepared to go anywhere at any time, or simply to wait around in case he is needed." [20]

Just as the commitment and spiritual worth of the Robinsons were judged by the extent to which they sacrificed their marriage relationship and their child's needs to the purposes of their group, the loyalty of the corporate manager is usually measured by the acceptance of corporation priorities over anything else in life.

Of course, corporations vary in their demands, and some managers sacrifice their family's interests over and above what the corporation requires. Personal ambition can take a toll without any pressure at all from corporate authority.

■   ■   ■

Studies of corporations generally recognized as continuously innovative, with long-term records of growth and profitability, indicate that a strong *corporate culture* is a key ingredient in their success. By corporate culture we mean a set of values or principles that permeate a company and form the guidelines for decision-making at all levels. [21] The inculcation of those values constitutes a process of corporate socialization that seems to be responsible for the survival from generation to generation of many large business organizations, providing stability and dependable responses. "What emerges in firms as different as AT&T is from Proctor and Gamble, as Morgan Guaranty is from IBM or Delta Airlines, is an awesome internal consistency which powerfully shapes behavior." [22]

For example, IBM teaches all employees its three "Basic Beliefs": 1) respect for the individual, 2) best possible service to our customers, 3) every task performed in a superior manner. Delta Airlines "Family Feeling" and AT&T's "Universal Service" are other examples of core values taught to all employees and taken seriously. Although the phrases sound like platitudes, within the corporation they are very meaningful.

These "significant meanings," "shared values," or "spiritual fabric" have been described as superordinate goals guiding the entire organization. They play a very practical role because employees must often make decisions on their own; as long as they are guided by the corporate shared values, decisions are likely to fit in with company policy.[23]

Achieving a strong corporate culture that managers really care about requires a process of indoctrination to convert a recruit to the corporation's point of view. Richard Pascale lists a number of steps in the process of "socialization," including "humility-inducing experiences."

> Humility inducing experiences in the first months on the job precipitate self-questioning of prior behavior, beliefs and values. A lowering of individual self-comfort and self-complacency promotes openness toward accepting the organization's norms and values.
>
> Most strong culture companies get the new hire's attention by pouring on more work than can possibly get done. IBM and Morgan Guaranty socialize extensively through training where "you work every night until 2:00 a.m. on your own material and then help others." . . . Humility tends to flourish under certain conditions; especially long hours of intense work that bring you to your limits. When vulnerability is high, one also becomes close to one's colleagues—and cohesiveness is intensified in pressure cooker environments where little opportunity is given to reestablish social distance and regain one's bearings . . . Near identical patterns of long hours, exhausting travel schedules and extensive immersion in case work are true at the major consulting firms and law practices.[24]

The use of overwork is also a feature of extreme cults, as in the case of Life Force. An ex-convert from the Unification Church described what it was like there:

> Sleep especially, was viewed as an indulgence since God never slept in His efforts to save mankind. Sleep, more than food, thus came to represent the most sought-after "privilege" of a future life in the Kingdom of Heaven. The staff averaged three hours a night; newer Family would average six. Recognized but unspoken was a state of constant exhaustion in all righteous children of God.[25]

Overwork is part of many initiations. Army recruits rise early and are put through long forced marches. Doctors during internship may get only one night's sleep every two days. Overwork facilitates submission through a kind of anesthesia produced by exhaustion; rebellion takes energy.[26] Immersion in the newly joined world to the exclusion of other influences is also important in initiations. Consider this description of how Schlumberger, until recently one of the most successful corporations of our time, initiates its engineers:

> Like military recruits who go through basic training together, they became a clan. They worked sometimes seven days a week for two straight months. They lived, ate, drank, showered, watched video cassettes, and vacationed together. They swapped stories about their work. For months at a time, the only people they had contact with worked for Schlumberger or for an oil company.[27]

The resemblance of such initiations to the procedures of religious cults is striking. That the resulting corporate attitude evokes from observers the phrase "religious fervor" is not surprising. Indeed, some executives are quite explicit about the parallel with religion:

> People need to believe in something larger than themselves. To be successful . . . a corporation must learn from the Japanese that "we have the responsibility that religion used to have." A good company must not be just a slave to profits; it must strive to perform a service and to beat its competitors. But more . . . it must measure itself against a higher standard, seeking perfection.[28]

Terrance Deal and Allen Kennedy, who studied the cultures of eighty corporations, also spoke of the corporate religion they had observed. "The Catholic church has something in common with IBM, Mary Kay, McDonald's, the Polaris project, the U.S. Forest Service, and countless numbers of other successful organizations—all of them capture some of the same religious tone."[29]

At the same time, as in the case of Life Force, high purposes may be subverted, with destructive results. Thomas Peters and Robert Waterman, authors of *In Search of Excellence*, warn that

> the more worrisome part of a strong culture is the ever present possibility of abuse. One of the needs filled by the strong ex-

cellent company cultures is the need most of us have for security. We will surrender a great deal to institutions that give
us a sense of meaning and, through it, a sense of security.[30]

Richard Pascale and Anthony Athos, who wrote *The Art of Japanese Management*, sound an even stronger cautionary note.

> Having made the case for the importance of superordinate
> goals in motivating employees and sustaining an organization
> over time, we must note that a skillful grasp of the use of all
> of our seven variables *can* be directed toward truly tragic out-
> comes. The staggering horror of the Third Reich and the mass
> suicides in Guyana come to mind. It is not hard to imagine an
> indoctrination of people into some kind of corporate Hitler
> Youth Corps.[31]

In the case of cults, moral principles are often violated to further the cult's success. The leader and the members justify immoral actions as being necessary for the greater good that the cult
will achieve: To make an omelet one must break eggs. Implied in
this attitude is an assumption that the leader's aims are sublimely
important, as is the welfare of the special group instrumental in
accomplishing these great goals. Also implied is a lowering of the
importance of any individual's welfare and a lowering still further
of the worth of the outsider. Part of the attraction of believing the
leader's views and actions to be of paramount importance is that
the follower's own sense of importance is heightened. One might
sense such a dynamic behind the arrogance and self-righteousness displayed by Oliver North at the Iran-contra hearings in 1987.
(In 1989, with Reagan out of office, North took a different role,
that of victim and scapegoat.)

Making the welfare of the corporation more important than
anything else, believing in its overriding importance, is the quali-
tative equivalent to a cult's belief in its divine mission. Charles
Wilson, former CEO of General Motors, put it succinctly in his
famous assertion, "What's good for General Motors is good for the
United States."

An appreciation of the power of cult dynamics may help us
understand immoral corporate actions by people who outside the
corporation conduct themselves differently. For example, according to Paul Brodeur (a *New Yorker* writer), the board of directors of

the Johns Mansville company deliberately withheld from their workers evidence that asbestos was dangerous to their health, asserting that there was no threat when they knew there was a very serious problem indeed.[32] Another writer, Morton Mintz, has described the actions of the A. H. Robbins Company in not withdrawing the Dalkon shield (a birth control device) from the marketplace after they had evidence of its serious side effects.[33] One reads of the failure of numerous nuclear power plants to correct safety problems. The list is long. I suggest that "the Corporation" evokes a fantasy of "the Big Parent" in the minds of the board of directors as well as in middle management. They identify with it and are reassured by it; the corporation is the protector and must be protected. Just as saving the world was used as a justification for the Life Force group's cruelty to its members or saving souls is used to justify unethical and illegal actions by religious zealots, so the economic well-being of the corporation may come to be considered important enough to justify actions that would otherwise be abhorred.

■   ■   ■

Psychologist Margaret Rioch has led many group meetings based on the Tavistock Group Relations Conference in which participants experience at first hand the power of authority-dependency relationships. She describes the participants' uncanny feeling as they realize how many of their own actions have been performed at the behest of the group's unconscious intentions:

> The sense of having a will of one's own, of being free to make one's own choice, disappears, and the individual experiences himself as a marionette pulled by the strings of the group or as being a channel through which the group pours its energy and expresses itself . . . The converse of the marionette phenomenon also occurs, especially in large groups, when an individual experiences himself as able to do anything with the group that he likes, sometimes so much so that he believes he *is* the group. This is often accompanied by a pseudo-religious fervor which carries the individual away into a grandiose sense of power. And this, too, is uncanny . . . These two ex-

periences, the sense of being all-powerful and the feeling of being a marionette, although they appear to be opposite, are essentially two sides of the same coin.[34]

Anyone who observes their own behavior will find many instances of compliance with one group or another. Furthermore, compliance becomes easier when we associate only with those who share our point of view. Then, hardly noticed, our window on reality may become so narrow that we cannot see the world, though we think we do.

Dependence on a Leader

A LL groups have leaders, and the primary family group is no exception. Whether the leader is formally recognized or not, someone makes the decisions, someone leads while the rest follow. The first leader we encounter is most likely to be a parent, usually our mother, the one who gives or withholds food, affection, praise, and security. Later, the father and/or other family members may take similar dominant positions in our life. Biological survival requires that we become adept at pleasing these powerful people, so as children we try to win their love and care, to avoid their wrath and control their comings and goings as best we can. As adults, we bring to other groups the attitudes and behaviors we learned so early, directing them toward new leaders who, in the psychological sense at least, stand above us. A cult leader exploits this tendency.

■   ■   ■

It is customary to think of cult leaders as powerful personalities who inspire, even hypnotize their audiences. Charismatic leaders from Mahatma Gandhi to Adolf Hitler have been described this way. But a cult leader need not be that impressive. Alex Monroe was cerebral, his discourses boring; he was intelligent but not inspiring. He developed power by distorting his followers' idealism, dividing their loyalties, using flattery, threats, and spurious logic to defeat objections and rationalize his demands. However, one particular characteristic links Alex with other cult leaders of greater charisma—he was authoritarian.

Authoritarians emphasize obedience, loyalty and the suppression of criticism. In the groups they lead, hierarchies of rank are emphasized and autonomy discouraged. (Sometimes such a leader takes a benign, "loving", tolerant position, but allows his or her lieutenants to enforce an authoritarian regime.)

Authoritarian leaders, especially, draw power from the dependency fantasy, from the individual's wish for an idealized parent. If we are sophisticated, we may reject, criticize, or look down on any public leader, but the wish remains, engendering seldom-noticed fantasies of someone (or something) who observes our behavior and rewards or punishes. It is not surprising that under certain conditions scepticism may be overthrown and conversion occur—as in the case of a prominent 60's radical who one day called a meeting and dismayed his admirers by announcing that he had become a follower of an Indian guru.

. . .

In our society, the tendency to look up to others while feeling small oneself is expressed in the enormous number of celebrities that clutter our minds. Statesmen, movie stars, sports figures, socialites, and the super-rich are given larger-than-life status by television and movies, by newspapers and magazines, all of which cater to this fantasy. (Sports are instructive to me, personally, in demonstrating how much I have embraced those images. Having watched football mainly on television, I have been shocked to go to a stadium and see how small the actual football field is and how mundane, ordinary and un-godlike the players are when not projected on a TV screen.)

Our predilection for inequality has even more prosaic expressions. Friends and patients alike remark that they do not feel now as they imagined their parents felt and as they still imagine "adults" feel. This misperception tends to isolate the aged. One evening, waiting for a table at a restaurant, I sat in the anteroom surrounded by grey-haired men and women, also waiting. I was struck by a sudden realization that these "oldsters" looked out at the world with the same youthful consciousness that I had. With that perception, the sense of separation from them that I had been feeling disappeared. I believe that "ageism" is not just fear of growing old, but also reveals the hidden wish to maintain a child's parental world.

. . .

We can trace our susceptibility to authoritarian leaders to the family structure, but in doing so we should not forget that the authoritarian character of the family is both functional and appropriate. Within the family parents and other elders are in fact superior in knowledge, experience, and strength to the children who depend on them for protection and satisfaction of needs. That parents command and children obey is realistic because of the large discrepancy in their respective capacities.

In a healthy family, as children mature and become more responsible and capable, the hierarchical, authoritarian structure moderates and becomes more democratic. Children are given appropriate responsibility and choice, which acts to reward competence and stimulate further growth. Eventually, the child's relationship to the parent reaches eye level psychologically as well as physically. This eye-level perspective is the hallmark of the mature adult. Such a perspective does not imply a denial of another's superior ability and knowledge; rather, feelings of appreciation and respect replace fear, awe, and dependency.

Just as the mature parent welcomes the child's ascent to equality and supports his or her maturation, the mature leader can and should exercise a similar function, according subordinates increasing responsibility, choice, and authority as they become capable. If this does not take place, subordinates remain in the position of children while the leader plays out the role of omnipotent parent. Thus, the key issue is not the strength of the leader, but the development or suppression of autonomy.

From this point of view, a hierarchical structure is not inherently bad; it can contribute to learning and is necessary when real differences in capacity exist. Furthermore, groups usually require a hierarchy for efficient performance of tasks. But a truly authoritarian leader is repressive and regressive.

■ ■ ■

The structure of cults is basically authoritarian; obedience and hierarchical power tend to take precedence over truth and conscience when they conflict, which they often do. Unfortunately, certain psychological benefits can make authoritarian groups very attractive—they provide the opportunity to feel protected and cared for. As noted earlier, the wish for parents does not disappear, but just goes underground when we become adults.

Mainstream politics provides many examples. Often, the key to a politician's popularity is the capacity to present the image of a strong, good parent, to convey an optimistic, sincere self-confidence, to communicate belief in a golden future. Apparent self-confidence and freedom from doubt are characteristics of all successful cult leaders because these postures resonate so strongly with the universal fantasy of a powerful, benign father or mother who will remove all difficulties and reassure the frightened child. As was widely remarked during Ronald Reagan's presidency, the capacity to evoke this image provides a leader with a "Teflon coating"; unpleasant, discordant facts about the leader's actions do not stick, are not held against him or her, but are pushed aside to preserve the good feelings he or she can arouse.

As adults most of us leave the conduct of public affairs to others whom we prefer to believe are superior in some way because to do so is less anxiety-producing. The reality may be quite different.

A poignant comment on this situation comes from an enterprising journalist, Craig Karpel, who gained access to the 1980 Bilderberg Meeting, held at Aachen, Germany. This exclusive, little-publicized summit conference of the West's power elite gathers every year to deal with whatever urgent problems face the United States and Western Europe. As Karpel points out, if the world were secretly run by someone or something, it would be the Bilderberg group. This particular meeting included David Rockefeller, Henry Kissinger, McGeorge Bundy, Helmut Kohl, Helmut Schmidt, Lord Home and a host of others comprising one hundred influential leaders in the fields of government, banking, publications, and industry from the various countries of the Western Alliance. The 1980 meeting took place at the beginning of a deep rift in European-American relations occasioned by Jimmy Carter's requests for sanctions against Iran and retaliation against the Soviet Union for the invasion of Afghanistan. There was also the matter of 16,000 Warsaw Pact tanks poised at the border of West Germany. The agenda for the meeting was entitled "America and Europe—Past, Present, and Future." Expecting that the men who ran things would plan a stealthy strategy of manipulation and control, dictating the future, Karpel was disappointed.

> One might imagine that the goal of Bilderberg must secretly be to attempt to shape future events and seek to profit from them. But in practice the purpose of the meetings is to assess what has already happened and to figure out how best to respond to it, with a view to hanging on to past gains.[1]

Karpel concluded that the participants were not leaders, but managers devoted to stability and self-preservation. He concluded:

> It is not inherently sinister to convene an assembly of wise men, led by those whom the wise believe to be the wisest. But one feels a certain queasiness when, like Dorothy's little dog, Toto, one pulls aside the curtain and discovers that wizards haven't the slightest idea what to do. To insinuate onself into such company, and to return then to the realm of roller disco and headphone radios, is like slipping up the spiral stairway of a transoceanic 747 and into the cockpit only to discover that there is no one there. The night is dark. A howling storm lies ahead. You descend to the main cabin. The dinner service has been concluded. A number of passengers are noisily airing petty complaints. The lights dim. The movie is about to begin . . .
> And so the secret, the hideous grisly secret of Bilderberg is revealed. There's nobody at the controls, folks. We're flying blind. Let's hope there's foam on the runway, friends and neighbors, 'cause we're coming in on a wing and a prayer.[2]

The driver's seat is empty, the parents have gone. But who wants to know?

▪ ▪ ▪

Looking up to a leader may be the result of a need to maintain a fantasy of the leader's superiority. Ronald Reagan was particularly attuned to fantasy's attractiveness to the public. James Barber, professor of political science at Duke University, commented in the *New York Times*:

> President Reagan's indifference to reality is hardly news. His criterion of validity is drama, not empiricism. As David Stockman, Director of the Office of Management and Budget, once summed up the White House system: "Every time one fantasy doesn't work they try another one." Mr. Reagan, told by a reporter that one of his favorite, endlessly repeated anecdotes— how a black hero at Pearl Harbor ended segregation in the armed forces—was total fiction, replied: "I remember the scene. . . . It was very powerful." What matters to him is the grace and theatrical force of a performance; as a lifelong practitioner of illusion, he is in no way embarrassed by its victory over the facts.[3]

As Barber goes on to note, the contradictions ignored by the public are striking indeed. Advocating law and order at home, Reagan violated international law and order by mining Nicaragua's waters. He blithely hailed dictators as "friends of democracy" and compared the Nicaraguan contras to the founding fathers of the United States. He secretly sold arms to a terrorist nation and lied about it when the story first broke. In the "Baby Jane Doe" case, the Reagan administration tried to force hospitals to care for hopelessly defective infants while cutting the federal funds hospitals would need to provide such special services. Similarly, Reagan opposed abortion and at the same time endeavored to slash the budgets of agencies that would provide care for unwanted infants. It didn't seem to matter. People regarded President Reagan as a nice guy, warm-hearted, sincere. He survived the Iran-contra debacle.

While Reagan's supporters ignored many of these contradictions to preserve the fantasy, his opponents erred in making Reagan a "bad father." Assigning him an evil capacity and intent, they often didn't consider that in believing his own fictions, willfully ignoring facts, rationalizing, accepting the reassurances of the friends who surrounded him, and preferring agreeable fantasies to disagreeable facts, Reagan behaved much like the rest of us. He didn't fool the public, he *was* the public, as other popular presidents before him have been. Those who hated him and those who loved him saw Reagan magnified, larger than themselves, and resisted an eye-level view.

Although Reagan has provided a particularly startling case of wishes dominating facts, the same process takes place in America with every president. And woe to him who falls from grace. It is interesting that the principal charge against Jimmy Carter was that he failed to provide leadership; yet he led brilliantly at Camp David. However, Carter did not appear decisive, confident, protective, optimistic; he was not, as one young woman put it about Ronald Reagan, "the father I always wanted." Jimmy Carter proved ordinary, like us, and I believe this was a major reason why voters felt he had to be replaced.

A leader's role is more complex than it might appear. As powerful as he or she might seem, a leader is also the captive of the group and may not fail the group's expectation or waver on the pedestal. If a leader does, the group may annihilate him. And so the eminence initially sought by the leader can become a prison; the tyrant is tyrannized. Leader and follower alike to some degree enact a dependency fantasy that requires an all-powerful parent who protects and rewards and a group of children who have no responsibilities other than obedience. The leader, as much as the group members, wishes to believe that an omnipotent, perfect parent is possible. And when a person assumes the mantle, he or she participates in the fantasy as faithfully as does the follower.

Yet it IS still a fantasy. Margaret Rioch comments that

> we do indeed long for a shepherd who will guide us into green and safe pastures. The trouble with this simile, when applied to human beings, is that the shepherd is another sheep. He may be dressed up in a long cloak and accompanied by a tall staff with a crook on the end of it or by other formidable symbols of high office. But underneath the cloak is one of the sheep, and not, alas, a member of a more intelligent and more far-seeing species. But the wish, and sometimes, the need, for a leader is so strong that it is almost always possible for one of the sheep to play the role of shepherd of the flock.[4]

■ ■ ■

Most people realize the danger a leader can pose; they have read of Jonestown and they know of the crimes of Stalin, Hitler, Mao Tse-tung, Pol Pot. The precariousness and danger of the leader role for the leader is not so well known, although it is illustrated by the face of many who have headed New Age religious and utopian groups.

For Alex Monroe, leader of the Life Force movement, the need to maintain the status of a superior, omnipotent being was a key factor. Carried away by grandiose wishes, Alex expanded his activities, publishing an ambitious magazine and establishing multiple training centers. At the same time, he was unwilling to share his power; he had to supervise and decide everything. Alex could not manage all these tasks, and he dealt with his failure by projecting blame on everyone; as a consequence, his paranoid thinking accelerated. It should be noted that his followers supported this process because they chose to overlook the contradictions between the mystical teachings he espoused and the dishonest cruel behavior he—and they—engaged in. For his followers, to recognize what was actually taking place would have been to cease to believe in Alex as a powerful, wise parent and themselves as his disciples/children pursuing an ennobling, special path. Neither Alex nor the group wished to give up the fantasy.

A study of history reveals numerous leaders overreaching themselves, becoming inflated with an omnipotent dream they share with their followers. Perhaps because of the behavior of their emperors, the ancient Romans had an awareness of the problem of grandiosity. As a victorious general on his day of triumph rode past the cheering crowds, leading a long procession of soldiers, captured slaves, and booty, a man would stand behind him in the chariot continually whispering, "Remember, you are mortal."

It is hard for a leader to remember that he or she is mortal when followers wish for a divinity, when they attribute to the leader the qualities of a superparent. In addition, the leader finds that he or she can wield enormous influence over group members through the gratification he or she can provide or withhold. That gratification is seen in its most intense form as "bliss," which in this context can be interpreted as the joy that springs up when an adult becomes a child once again. How wonderful to relinquish all choice and decision, to be secure in the belief that the superparent will take care of everything. When, at the same time, this regression is said to be for the good of the human race, to help bring about the salvation of the world, then the bliss is complete because it seems noble as well.

■   ■   ■

Of course, it takes some doing to maintain the fantasy of riding in the back seat of the car. Frequently, I find that a patient has refused to exercise his or her full strength, fearing the loss of a feeling of protection, of being watched over by a parental force (even a cruel one) that stands between him or her and an imagined chaos. This tendency is widespread.

When a leader's actions conflict with the group's principles, standards, or values, followers may twist words and meanings to reduce cognitive dissonance and maintain the fantasy. According to published accounts, one well-known Eastern guru with a propensity for drunkenness became angered at a visiting couple who had withdrawn from a wild party (held during a retreat) and secluded themselves in their room, refusing his commands to appear. He ordered his guards to bring them by force—which they did, breaking down the door and engaging the man in a fight during which he wielded broken glass as a weapon, wounding one of the guards. The couple was finally brought to stand before the guru, who then ordered that they be stripped naked. The woman and man were thrown to the floor and their clothes torn off. The woman called for help but only one onlooker came to their defense (and he was struck). The nude couple were then brought to stand before the guru. Shortly thereafter, everyone at the party stripped. The guru's actions were later justified by a follower: ". . .vajrayana teachings are ruthless; compassion takes many forms."[5]

Calling the drunken guru's behavior compassion is an example of what George Orwell, in 1984, called double-speak, manipulating the abstractions of language to suggest a meaning and value opposite to the real situation. This is one way discrepancies between group fantasies and actual behavior can be painted over.

The power of the dependency fantasy is underscored in the case cited above by the fact that the abused couple chose to stay on for the conclusion of the retreat. The man explained, "We'd come to study the whole course; we'd taken it (as he [the guru] knew) seriously; we wanted to finish what we'd begun, and not be scared off. The last lap, about to begin, was the famous Tantric teachings."[6]

In such extreme cases, the individual's perception has to be narrowed and critical thinking suppressed. Groups have effective means of doing this. As in Clara Robinson's case, if a group member voices objections or criticism, he or she may be attacked as ignorant, unworthy, selfish, elitist—whatever term is used to define badness. Groups, as well as leaders, may punish dissent or deviation when maintenance of the superparent fantasy requires that no imperfections be revealed lest the whole structure be put in jeopardy. Seldom does anyone stand behind the leader to whisper, Remember, you are mortal.

In a cult the leader is accepted as having special powers and/ or semidivine status which places him or her outside the behavior norms of the ordinary person. As we have seen, similar exemption from the rules and the accompanying claim to infallibility enables many a leader to perform unethical acts that would otherwise not be countenanced. In ordinary life traces of this dynamic can be seen, although the situation is seldom as stark as in extreme cults.

When facts become impossible to ignore, the leader is dethroned; but all too often the dependency fantasy continues; a new "parent" is found.

We find examples of the abuses of the role of leader in recent political history. Richard Nixon's handling of the Watergate break-in suggests that being president had eroded his judgment, encouraged grandiosity, and blinded him with the righteousness which arises easily in powerful leaders when they are criticized and challenged. For absolute rulers the danger is even worse; witness the career of Idi Amin, who ended up rivaling Caligula in the bloody, paranoid expressions of his vanity and fear.

．　　■　　■

We have seen how the idealism of Hugh and Clara was used as a lever to break their ties with family members and to justify unethical, harmful actions. Idealism can be exploited as a source of a leader's power; he or she need only inspire and mobilize the readiness for self-sacrifice which exists within many people.

In the business world, the importance of generating fervor was noted by Thomas Peters and Robert Waterman, Jr., in their studies of "excellent" companies. They found that "transforming leadership" played a crucial role in the history of outstanding corporations; charismatic leaders stirred the emotions of their employees so as to instill a sense of elevated purpose, fulfilling the crucial human need for meaning and purpose.

Sometimes the meaning may not seem very profound to an outside observer. Charles Edward Wilson, president of General Electric from 1940 to 1950, created a strong impression on Reginald Jones (who himself later became president of the company).

> I still remember Charlie Wilson, the very epitome of the inspirational leader. He told us, in the Town Hall, how Westinghouse planned to surpass us in sales and earnings. 'They should live so long!' he roared. 'Their grandchildren should live so long.' And then he got us out behind the marching band, and they led us out to the flagpole playing 'Onward Christian Soldiers.' At that moment, I would have followed him anywhere on earth—and beyond if necessary.[7]

Even if the summons is for political or economic goals rather than religious ones, the energies mobilized will be the same and the final result is declared to be for the greater good, creating paradise on earth, saving the world. What matters is that people's deepest desires for the Good be mobilized. That is why the most effective leaders inspire rather than overpower. This was the conclusion of a study of audience reactions to a charismatic leader:

> They were apparently strengthened and uplifted by the experience; they felt more powerful, rather than less powerful or submissive. This suggests that the traditional way of explaining the influence of a leader on his followers has not been entirely correct. He does not force them to submit and follow him by the sheer overwhelming magic of his personality and persuasive powers . . . he is influential by strengthening and inspiriting his audience.[8]

Anyone who has watched films of Hitler's speeches and the crowds' reactions would agree. Hitler, transformed by his own fantasies, brought his audience's fantasies and wishes to life, made them seem possible. He whipped his listeners to intoxicating heights of emotion, restoring significance to their lives, asking for sacrifices.

Most of us need to feel that our lives have meaning and purpose, that we are special and are living in a way that is consonant with our ideals. And it is not only the young that long to live idealistically, older people who have led practical lives and have accepted the necessity of compromising their ideals may respond with great commitment if offered the opportunity to sacrifice for a good cause. This appeal to the perception of a larger reality, to unsatisfied idealism and the wish for meaning can be very powerful, and it can be put to good or bad use.

■   ■   ■

Authoritarian leadership tends to become established in large corporations where power has become overly centralized. Harold Geneen, who ran ITT like a potentate, knows whereof he speaks: "The authority vested in the chief executive of a large company is so great, so complete, and the demands made upon his time are so consuming, that most chief executives slip into authoritarian roles without realizing that the process is going on."[9]

John De Lorean, former General Motors executive, describes the increase in authoritarianism at General Motors in the years following the departure of Alfred Sloan, who had been chairman of the board:

> I watched GM's operations slowly become centralized. The divisions gradually were stripped of their decision-making power . . . The guiding corporate precept of centralized policymaking and decentralized decision making was totally and purposefully ignored . . . There was no system of checks and balances. The divisions reported to The Fourteenth Floor. But The Fourteenth Floor reported only to itself.[10]

The authoritarian attitude results in an emphasis on punishment and the manifestation of power by saying no. The veto is safer and more impressive than granting permission. Although innovation and creativity may be given lip service, even insignificant mistakes are usually punished despite their being the inevitable price of developing a new approach or a new product.[11]

Peters and Waterman, in reviewing the problem, came to the conclusion that this behavior reflects the same superior/inferior perspective that Erich Fromm emphasized in his study of authoritarian political behavior.[12] "Central to the whole notion . . . is the superior/subordinate relationship, the idea of manager as 'boss,' and the corollary that orders will be issued and followed. The threat of punishment is the principle implied power that underlies it all."[13]

The hierarchical emphasis is underlined by corporate class distinctions. The executive washroom, the special dining room for upper management, superior furnishings and more space are all indicators of a higher position. Indeed, the top executives usually will be found on the highest floor. This institutionalization of the upward gaze is accepted almost everywhere and seldom questioned any more than is the assumption of parents having the largest bedroom in the home, a separate bathroom, and other special prerogatives.

Even when the chief executive officer wishes to make the organization less authoritarian, the task is not easy. Cornelle Maier, former CEO for Kaiser Aluminum recalls a lesson he learned when his corporation began to decentralize decision making.

> As we started giving more authority to our operating divisions an interesting thing happened . . . all of the managers working for me felt that they should have a lot more authority in their decision-making: capital spending, personnel moves— what have you. That wasn't a surprise. What was a surprise was that nearly all of them felt that the people working for them *shouldn't* have more authority! . . . They wanted a lot more authority but they didn't want to give that authority away.[14]

Nor did they wish to give up the symbols of elevated status they had acquired as part of the superior/inferior authoritarian world.

●   ●   ●

The chief executive officer of a large corporation does not usually claim divine attributes. However, the CEO's power to hire, fire, reward, and punish is very great and in the hands of an authoritarian personality this power can result in a suppression of critical thinking within the corporation and a mindless conformity and fawning support for whatever the CEO believes and decides to do. Sometimes this behavior extends to a slavish copying of the style of dress and behavior of the boss. In his book, *The Fanciest Dive*, Christopher Byron gives an amusing description of the antics that took place at Time, Inc. when a new boss, Richard Munro, entered the scene:

> No sooner did word spread that the company's new president ate breakfast early most mornings at the Dorset Hotel on West Fifty-fourth Street than numerous subordinates began doing the same. It was there, one hot September morning in 1982 that Munro, having breakfast, stood up and removed his suit jacket to be more comfortable; all around the room Time Inc. executives promptly rose and did the same. . . . And when Munro took to carrying a red bandana with a corner flapping loosely from his hip pocket, the corridors of the Big House were soon ablaze with red bandanas waving jauntily from the hip pockets of hopeful executives.[15]

Like similar leaders everywhere, authoritarian executives can easily end up valuing the conformity, loyalty, obedience, and subservience of subordinates more than actual performance. A boss wants to trust his or her subordinates, to count on their loyalty, to know they fit in and will not cause trouble. Subordinates who conform to the boss's own style of dress and behavior evoke in him a sense of support and comfort. The boss feels he knows where his subordinates stand and can rely on them to perform as he would in unsupervised situations. In turn, the employees know that salaries, promotion, and assignments within the company lie in the hands of their boss. When obedience, loyalty, and conformity matter more than performance, cult-like behavior takes place all along the hierarchy. Secrecy about salaries, competition for the boss's favor, and fear of being left behind can create an atmosphere reminiscent of that which occurred in Life Force. One manager described

> A big fear complex that operates within GPI because there are so many people who are, or will, or might be your boss, or might be or do have an influence on you one way or the other.

The fear syndrome keeps you from speaking up and it works in the compensation area as well. While you may know your salary, obviously more money is at the whimsical beck and call of your boss and his boss and a few other people perhaps.[16]

■   ■   ■

What is a god if not a supreme authority? In religions the world over, the devout acknowledge their god's divine wisdom, mercy and awesome power; they pray for protection, forgiveness, and benefits. Even in Buddhism, whose founder declared that notions of gods and heavens were illusions, most believers bow to a Buddha idol with all the expectations found in theistic religions.

Few people take seriously the injunctions of mystics against seeking to understand the Ultimate via familiar images. Typical of such an injunction is the statement of Saint John of the Cross:

That inward wisdom is so simple, so general and so spiritual that it has not entered into the understanding enwrapped or clad in any form or image subject to sense, it follows that sense and imagination (as it has not entered through them nor has taken their form and color) cannot account for it or imagine, so as to say anything concerning it, although the soul be clearly aware that it is experiencing and partaking of that rare and delectable wisdom.[17]

Saint John maintained that knowledge of God cannot be expressed in terms of this world, cannot be articulated by using the images and concepts of everyday life: family, mother, father, children, reward, punishment, etc. Similar statements about the unknowability of the Godhead have been made by mystics of widely differing cultures throughout history. They are very consistent. Nevertheless, formal religions tend to use the familiar relationship of parent and child as the model for a human being's relationship to the divine. This model inevitably creates cult dynamics in religious organizations. In part, the problem arises because the founding mystics of the theistic religions, in their attempts to communicate the ineffable, made use of the concept of God the Father, the supreme parent, although only as a metaphor. However, their listeners took the meaning literally. Thus, religions end up teaching, Be good (obey God's wishes) and you will be rewarded (enter heaven or nirvana); if you are bad (disobey God) you will be punished (with hell or reincarnation).

The dependency wish usually requires tangible authority figures and they are seldom in short supply. Mohammed abolished the priesthood but equivalent ecclesiastical officials, the mullahs, arose after his death and in some areas, such as Iran (now a theocracy), the chief mullah rules with more authority than the present-day Pope. Another example is provided by Hinduism. Although the Upanishads preach the oneness of all being, the Brahmin priests whose function it is to transmit Hindu teaching have maintained the caste system and their superior status within it. It took all the power of Gandhi to begin to crack the caste barriers enclosing the untouchables of India.

Theistic religions, such as Christianity, Judaism, or Islam, are intrinsically authoritarian, expressing the belief in God as a Supreme Being who transcends the material world, is infinitely superior to human beings, and to whom we owe obedience. God's absolute superiority in power, goodness, and knowledge may be used by religious leaders to justify their own authority and to legitimize their demands for submission. For the most part, theistic religions teach that compliance with God's will, coupled with an appropriately humble attitude, will be rewarded by protection and help for the supplicant: that pride (putting oneself at eye level with God) is a sin and submission a virtue. The greater the emphasis on the supreme god (the superparent) versus the inferior follower (the child), the more the stage is set for cult behavior in any religion, orthodox or not.

Thus, as in any authoritarian system, the basic perspective of most religious groups is one of superior/inferior relationships; as obedience is the prime virtue in all authoritarian systems, so obedience to God's commandments is a prime virtue in theistic religions. This is espoused most rigidly by fundamentalists, those who believe in the literal, inerrant truth of the Bible, the Koran, or any other religious text. Rev. Jerry Falwell puts the matter most unequivocally: "We must be obedient to the Word of God. Obedient. Whatsoever He sayeth unto you, do it! That's all there is to it! Find out what God is saying to you and obey Him. Obey the Lord. Obedience!"[18]

Of course, the critical issue is not obedience, per se, but why we are obedient and to what or to whom. Blind obedience leads to totalitarianism, refusal to obey anything leads to chaos. Free will (as distinguished from impulsivity) combines obedience with choice; it is "the experience of being the author of the law you obey."[19] Being the author means to *choose* the values expressed in the law, to freely assent to them based on one's judgment, experience, and sense of the Good.

The best religious leaders teach that a truly spiritual choice is an expression of one's self and not an expression of fear (of punishment), or greed (for reward), or vanity (being one of the chosen few). A story from the Sufic tradition, here told by Idries Shah, addresses this issue.

Three Reasons

There was once a powerful conqueror who had become emperor of a vast territory peopled by representatives of several beliefs.

His counselors said, "Great king, a deputation of thinkers and priests from each persuasion, is awaiting audience. Each hopes to convert you to the way of thinking of his school. We are in a quandary, because we cannot advise you to accept the ideology of one part, since it would alienate the goodwill of all the rest."

The king, for his part, said, "Neither is it fitting that a king should adopt beliefs for political reasons, and without thought for his own higher dignity and well-being."

The discussions continued for several hours, until a wise dervish, who had attached himself to the king's retinue many months before and had been silent ever since, stepped forward.

"Majesty," he said, "I am prepared to advise a course in which the interests of all parties will be safeguarded. The applicants will be abashed, the courtiers will be relieved of their anxiety to find a solution, the king will be able to retain his reputation for wisdom, and nobody will be able to say that he holds sway over the king's thoughts."

The dervish whispered his formula into the royal ear, and the king called the deputation to enter the throne-room.

Receiving the clerics and thinkers with all courtesy, the king said to them:

"I shall hear first of all the arguments of those among you who do not say 'Believe or you are in peril'; or 'Believe because it will give you happiness', or 'Adopt my beliefs because you are a great king.'"

The applicants dispersed in confusion.[20]

Although a person may be drawn to a religion through the wish to find meaning and purpose, to serve God and humanity, religious organizations all too often fail to avoid stimulating fear, greed, or flattery in recruiting members. Consequently, the obedience commanded tends to evoke the attitude of the child toward its parent. Obedience is certainly necessary for certain kinds of learning and development, and has a definite function in religious instruction, but great religious teachers agree that the highest obedience is to the religion's essence.

Obedience to the literal scriptures, to the form rather than the essence, opens the door to cult processes. This problem of form taking precedence over content is one that plagues all religions and is defined as idolatry. Anything can be idolized, including rules and rituals, and the resulting behavior may contradict the values that the religion espouses. A Benedictine prioress reflected on the reversal of priorities that marked religious life during her early years with the order:

> Formalism and legalism had completely replaced either spiritual direction or blessing. Every day life got smaller. Religious life had become the celebration of the trivial. While McCarthyism raged, I was told to guard myself from spiritual distraction by not listening to the news. While Martin Luther King began black sit-ins of white lunch counters in a country that routinely lynched blacks, I believed it when they said that had nothing to do with religious life and concentrated on darning my socks, a real sign of poverty, I was told.[21]

When a religion's texts are regarded as literally true and infallible, a likely next step is that the leader's interpretation becomes what is true and sacred. Then a member's obedience is transferred to the priest, rabbi, mullah, or minister; this is the lowest level of obedience, most likely to lead to overt cult behavior. Rev. R. G. Puckett, the Baptist evangelist who heads Americans United, warned of this development taking place in American Christian fundamentalist churches.

> The church is centered in the pastor. He *is* the authority, the ruling force. Falwell, Robison, Robertson, all the rest—these are personality cults. People follow the person, the pastor, not Jesus Christ. He may say he is not telling anyone how to vote or how to live, but the very climate and mentality of the whole church says: what the pastor wants is what we do.[22]

Such preachers do not claim divinity, only that God speaks to them, inspires them, guides them. That claim may be quite enough to demand complete obedience and to brand disagreement with their views and wishes as a sign that the defiant member is lost to salvation.

Religious leaders may be as attracted to the security of certainty and surrender as are their followers. Many really believe they are commanded by God, that they have become instruments of his will, and that their pronouncements are beyond error. Others with less exalted views of themselves nevertheless succumb to the lure of certainty and rightness. From a priest who has faced the shortcomings of his church we have an eloquent testimony to that attraction:

> I do not [now] live without worry or responsible concern. In fact, I have never felt so responsibile since I discovered that the Church cannot absorb my conscience, nor replace my mind. Life was easier when I knew where everything fit, when I could lose myself in the structure of a massive organization. There heaven and hell were governed by careful laws. There God's friendship was certain and manageable, and I was satisfied when I kept the Church's rules.[23]

Liz Harris, writing in the *New Yorker*, contrasted her own state of uncertainty with the security of the Hasidic world.

> I envied them their sureness and the sheer weight it gave them. I had, of course, my family, my friends, my work, and the various pleasures that came my way, but spiritually I felt

as if I floated weightlessly in the universe. The Hasidim had a world without time, eternal life, and the extraordinary sense that everything they did counted.[24]

. . .

Surrender is a basic feature of the spiritual life. As an acceptance of selfless goals in place of self-centeredness, it is something most recognize as inherently desirable. Yet the call to surrender can become a tool for manipulation and control when critical judgment is set aside. As we have seen earlier, Clara Robinson was exhorted to give up her concern for her child and surrender to Life Force's greater spiritual task as set forth by Alex Monroe. Her reluctance to do so was defined as selfishness. Barbara Underwood, a former Moonie, described similar coercion in the Unification Church,[25] and total surrender is called for by fundamentalist preachers and organizations such as the Campus Crusade. Bill Bright, writing in *Jesus and the Intellectual* makes it quite explicit: "The secret is surrender. Commitment to Christ involves the surrender of the intellect, the emotions and the will—the total person."[26]

There is no place in such groups for reasoned, independent judgment; no free will, no responsible choice, only literal adherence to sacred text as selected and interpreted by the church leader or organization. With surrender, the authority of the leader is maximized, the follower feels relieved of uncertainty and choice and can then experience the "bliss" of someone who has "returned home."

. . .

Since most of the examples I have cited are from the fundamentalist and conservative wings of established religions, some readers may feel my conclusions do not apply to them because they are involved in less doctrinaire, more moderate, more sophisticated beliefs and practices. I would respond that it is a matter of degree and that each person needs to assess the extent to which cult behavior and the dependency fantasy are operative in his or her religious life.

I believe that such awareness is of particular importance because the goal of religion should be to facilitate the direct experience of the spiritual dimension. Although human beings carry
within them the potential for regressive dependency, they also
contain the potential for the intuition of the spiritual—that perception, however dim, of something that transcends the reality
accessible to the senses and ordinary thought. This intuition is
universal and can be very powerful.[27]

Indeed, mystics claim that spiritual development consists of
strengthening that inborn intuitive capacity, permitting one to
"know" the larger reality called Truth, God, Original Mind,
Brahma—whatever name may be invoked.[28] Assuming the exis-
tence of that perceptual capacity, latent in everyone, the question
arises of the effect of cult-like behavior on one's capacity to experience the spiritual.

Study of the mystical literature of many religions reveals all
these traditions to be in agreement that to develop the ability to
perceive God or Truth, one must shift from a self-centered orientation to serving the underlying reality. This service must be without concern for personal gain; basic intentions must change.
There can be no cheating on this one because motivation deter-
mines the form of consciousness. You cannot grasp the spiritual
world as you can the material since a "grasping" mind is necessarily focused on discrete objects and cannot encompass a world of
connectedness, of unity. It is for this reason—a functional, not a
moral reason—that mystics assert that no matter what you may
say or do, no matter how you may appear, if your underlying intention is self-centered, perception of Truth or God is impossible.
The necessary shift in motivation takes time, effort, and skillful
guidance. To "repent and believe" is not enough.

An organization that enhances selfish intentions is at cross
purposes with spiritual development; it is anti-spiritual.[29] To stimulate fear of punishment, greed for reward, or vanity at being
among the saved versus the damned, is to stimulate a self-
centered orientation. These powerful motivations are not in the
service of spiritual development. This is why one saint declared:

O Lord!
   If I worship you from fear of hell, cast me into hell.
   If I worship you from desire for paradise, deny me para-
dise.[30]

Dependence on a leader/parent can be doubly destructive in the sphere of religion. Not only does it impair ordinary judgment and create a regressive pull on members and converts of religious groups, it prevents them from progressing beyond a self-centered orientation. This blocks the perception of the spiritual force that is the vital element within religions, a force that might otherwise enhance and guide their lives.

I do not mean to say that a religion's members may not devote themselves to actions benefitting others. To the contrary, great charity and service have been inspired by religious beliefs and administered by religious institutions throughout the centuries. Cult behavior is largely an interior problem in which form (doctrine and authority) dominates content (the experience of the Real), producing idolatry. Understanding the nature of the problem facilitates an attitude vitally different from the authoritarian. A School Sister of Notre Dame comments,

> Although as a woman religious I am identified with church institutions, in the final analysis, God, not any institution, is paramount. To associate with and to preserve any structure at the expense of serving God and humankind is idolatry. To follow God's call rather than an institutional call, if the two are in conflict, is a moral imperative. I pray always for the grace and the insight to discern God's call.[31]

Certainly, if a religious group provides us with security and identity, we will not see its cult features very readily. One's own group is thought to be above such behavior; a cult is seen as something that you yourself don't belong to. But perhaps in some ways you do. It just isn't obvious when measured against Jonestown or the Life Force Institute.

. . .

My own profession of psychiatry is not immune from cult behavior. To begin with, the psychotherapeutic situation itself encourages the emergence of a dependency relationship. In psychoanalysis and analytically oriented psychotherapy, the therapist reveals almost nothing while the patient is expected to reveal all.

Since the therapist is calm, reticent, and an authority while the patient is distressed and seeking help, a parent/child feeling quickly develops. With time, the unique character of the patient's early relationship to his or her parent or parents tends to be transferred to the therapist. In fact Freud emphasized the importance of this transference in helping the patient and saw the intensification of the parent/child fantasy as a desired effect of the psychotherapeutic situation.

Nevertheless, it should be recognized that Freud intended that the patient reclaim the power he or she bestowed on the therapist. He hoped that analysis of the transference would give to the patient an eye-level perspective toward the analyst, as well as toward others. I know of no other profession or institution that has established a goal of relinquishing authority and built in comprehensive techniques for its accomplishment. Even though the return of power takes place only imperfectly (and in some cases not at all), dedication to an eye-level relationship is a direct counter to cult-like behavior and offers hope for a more mature society.

Regrettably, the ideal may be preached but not always practiced. Psychotherapists may exploit their position in the same fashion as do cult leaders. This can take place in several ways, from automatically interpreting a patient's criticism as neurotic, dismissing any questioning as projection or acting out of the transference, to outright sexual seduction. I remember a cartoon about psychiatry with the punch line "This is the only business where the customer is always wrong."

The patient is *not* always wrong in his or her perceptions of the therapist. It is crucial that the therapist be able to see in what ways the patient is correct, acknowledge and support the patient's perception and go on to investigate what the therapist's error or limitation means to the patient. Competent therapists do this, but only an ideal therapist is completely free from defensiveness and denial.

Therapists, like other leaders, often are flattered and idealized by their patients, who wish them to be omnipotent, omniscient, surrogate parents. Resisting this seduction is particularly hard for a psychotherapist because he or she is likely to have entered the profession with the very fantasy of being an ideal parent, one who "saves" grateful patients. (In this context, the patient may represent the therapist as a child or the therapist's parent, whoever needed saving.) Having become a therapist, one may fall in with the patient's wish when it supports the saviour fantasy. While the patient is not officially a follower, nor is the therapist a cult leader, the dependency needs of the former and the omnipotent fantasies of the latter can create cult-like behavior.

Actual cults may develop in therapeutic situations. Although this is rare, there have been instances of therapists who develop relationships with their patients in which they occupy the roles of colleagues, teachers, lovers, friends, and employers simulataneously. Such a violation of professional ethics and psychiatric principles is not necessarily due to substandard psychiatric training. In one study of five such "therapeutic cults," two of the leaders were psychoanalysts, members of the prestigious American Psychoanalytic Association, yet these therapeutic cults functioned almost like religious cults.[32] Although actual cult formation by psychiatrists is unusual, there are two areas where covert cult-like behavior is significant.

In the 1950s and 1960s, psychoanalysis was in its heyday of acceptance and power. The heads of departments of psychiatry in medical schools were usually psychoanalysts; it was assumed that the best psychiatry residents would become psychoanalysts—the second-best would have to settle for something inferior. Indeed, as a psychiatric resident, I was told that only psychoanalysis offered a patient real change, real treatment; psychotherapy was a patch-up job. (How powerfully such a consensus prevailed and affected judgment is hard to convey, even though there were abundant cases of unresolved neurotic problems among former analysands and among the training analysts themselves, and although one heard anecdotes of psychotherapy results that rivaled the best of psychoanalysis.) This assumption pervades much of the psychoanalytic literature today and I think it has had a debilitating effect on psychoanalytic thinking.

Psychoanalytic institutes, where psychoanalysis is taught, are not cults, but cult behavior does take place in them. Cult features have been so prominent that noted analysts have remarked on the similarity between psychoanalytic institutes and religious organizations. Otto Kernberg, training analyst at the Columbia University Center for Psychoanalytic Training and Research, points to features of psychoanalytic education that justify its designation as a system of religious beliefs:

> The religious assertion of faith in the existence of the deity and the essentially irrational nature of such a faith are not unlike the sense of conviction about the truth of psychoanalytic theory, particularly about the unconscious. This sense of conviction is usually traced to an emotional experience connected with the discovery of the unconscious in oneself and the experience of psychological change following this discovery. In both instances a highly subjective personal experience, an emotional encounter with the unknown rather than rational analysis, constitutes the anchoring pillar of the educational program.[33]

This could be a description of Hugh and Clara Robinson's conversion to faith in life force psychology, or of the experiences of converts to the numerous new religions of the sixties and seventies. Kernberg goes on to point out further similarities:

> In addition, this deeply transforming emotional experience is carried out in the context of an intense relation to another person, idealized and experienced as a spiritual guide . . . complemented by other mentors who focus on the limitations, shortcomings, mistakes, and inadequacies of the student's performance, while sustaining the assumption that they are working at a higher level, which the student must reach through ongoing self-exploration as well as learning about the formulations of the masters, in the end, the original master of the school, Freud.[34]

The analogy to religion is seconded by Jacob Arlow, a past president of the American Psychoanalytic Association, who pointed out that psychoanalytic education is unique among learned disciplines in that most of its basic texts are fifty years old. He observes that this can't be wholly explained as the debt of psychoanalysis to Freud because of a characteristic clinging to the past that marks the educational emphasis. Freud's earlier writings receives greater attention than either his later (superceding) writings or the contributions of recent analysts.[35] Arlow further notes that psychoanalytic training is experienced as a prolonged initiation rite.

> During a long course of tests which the initiates undergo (personal analysis, admission to courses, first case, second case, etc., graduation), the training analysts serve the double function characteristic of all initiators. Some intimidate the candidates; others act as sponsors and guides . . . anxiety propels the candidate into effecting an identification with the aggressor; the initiate remodels himself after the image the community holds up as the ideal.[36]

The situation of the candidates is not unlike that of members of Life Force who were dependent on the good opinion of leader/therapist Alex for their graduation to the inner circle of the Center. Depending on the candidate, the effects could easily be similar in kind.

■   ■   ■

In 1961 John F. Kennedy made the disastrous decision to go ahead with a covert invasion of Cuba by anti-Castro exiles, an operation commonly referred to afterwards as the Bay of Pigs. It was a spectacular failure. About a year later, when it was discovered that Russian nuclear missiles were being installed in Cuba, Kennedy was successful in bringing about their withdrawal, an operation usually called the Cuban Missile Crisis. Because the Bay of Pigs and the Cuban Missile Crisis were historic events whose decision-making processes are exceptionally well documented, I will use them to illustrate both cult behavior and the possibility of more realistic behavior at the government level.

Irving Janis, a psychologist who studied the effect of group process on presidential advisory groups, pointed to the important role of shared illusions in disasters such as the attempted invasion of Cuba. One was "the illusion of invulnerability." People believe that if their leader and everyone else thinks a proposal will succeed, then it will, even if it is risky and requires luck.

An air of omniscience and invulnerability is fostered by political leaders as well, in part because the public demands leaders

who are forceful and confident; unwavering optimism is preferred
to doubts and uncertainty. The fantasy of invulnerability is identical in cults, where it may lead to disaster. For example, an epo-
chal celebration, brainchild of a young Indian guru, was held
some years ago in Houston, Texas. With the guru's approval, his
followers hired the Astrodome, expecting to fill it with thousands
of people who would be drawn there to hear his message. Confidence was unbounded, no doubts were heard, as the guru was
presumed infallible. Publicity and preparations were extensive
and lavish, media coverage nation-wide. The celestial appearance
of the comet Kahootek was interpreted as a cosmic herald of the
grand event. What actually took place was a grand fiasco; although droves of the guru's followers arrived at the stadium, very
few others availed themselves of the opportunity to adulate him
and share in the momentous event. The monetary and public relations losses were staggering; the organization went into decline.

From the blissful, blind optimism of this guru and his followers to the arrogant overconfidence of top U.S. government officials
in the Bay of Pigs advisory group was not such a large step. Robert Kennedy recalled, "It seemed that, with John Kennedy leading
us and with all the talent he had assembled, *nothing could stop
us.*"[37]

Arthur Schlesinger felt the same.

> One further factor no doubt influenced him [John F. Ken-
> nedy]: the enormous confidence in his own luck. Everything
> had broken right for him since 1956. He had won the nomi-
> nation and the election against all the odds in the book. Every-
> one around him thought he had the Midas touch and could
> not lose. Despite himself, even this dispassionate and skepti-
> cal man may have been affected by the soaring euphoria of the
> new day.[38]

One cannot understand the phenomenon of authoritarian behavior in democratic presidents without appreciating the attraction for both leaders and followers of a superior/inferior, parent/
child perspective.

I have a vivid memory of an incident that occurred during a
Tavistock Group Relations Conference. Participants were divided
into several large groups and each group was asked to relate to
the other groups by appointing suitably empowered representa-

tives. No group leaders were designated, no goals or structure provided. In the absence of authority and direction, anxiety built up rapidly. Everyone talked at once. I tried to reduce the chaos by establishing leadership. "Make me leader!" I pleaded. The group would not appoint any one to that power position. The disorganization and tension increased. Finally, I stood up; shouted, "I'm taking command!" and began appointing people to assume the functions of doorkeeper, ambassador, and so forth. The same people who would not voluntarily delegate authority now obeyed with alacrity. The conference conditions had intensified our primitive impulses and we behaved like a group of sibling children, no one willing to take the adult action of delegating power. When my discomfort drove me to take the role of dictator/parent the others readily submitted, for they were then freed of responsibility.

A parallel need—to structure a situation in terms of a child rebelling against a bad parent—was illustrated, for me, when I had to hospitalize an adolescent against his will. A state trooper arrived at my office to take him away. It was clear that the officer wanted to be compassionate and helpful. My patient would have none of this. He resisted, struggled, taunted, and provoked the trooper until the man became angry and, finally, cuffed him on the head with his open hand. Immediately, the young man became docile and accompanied him readily. It was clear to me that my patient had succeeded in his aim of making the policeman a "bad parent." Later, a teacher at the boy's school denounced this "police brutality" and was indignant when I replied that I thought the state trooper was the one who had been brutalized.

In each of these incidents, those involved refused or were unable to go beyond the child/parent relationship, and insisted on an authoritarian structure. I see the compliance of the first instance and the rebelliousness of the second as two aspects of looking up at authority.

∎　∎　∎

Like most cults and formal religions, governments cite a higher principle or authority to justify their actions. (This is probably what Samuel Johnson mocked when he said, "Patriotism is the last refuge of the scoundrel.") As Alex Monroe's lies were justified as being necessary to advance the work of saving the world, other cult leaders, tyrants, and terrorists invariably defend immoral and violent actions as serving God or truth or country or freedom.

Psychologist Stanley Milgram's research demonstrated the effectiveness of this reference to a higher authority. People from all walks of life participated as subjects in his studies. An experimenter in a grey lab coat told the subjects that the purpose of the experiment was to advance science, and then instructed them to give increasing electric shocks to a "learner" strapped into an electric chair. (Unbeknownst to the subjects, the learner was a confederate of the researchers and actually received no shocks at all.) The subjects were told that although the shocks could be extremely painful to the learner, they caused no permanent damage.

As the experiment proceeded, the learner became increasingly vocal, agitated, and desperate, and eventually screamed each time the subject shocked him. He demanded and begged to be released, expressing concern for his heart. Most subjects showed evidence of considerable stress as they were ordered to continue despite the anguished cries of pain, which they could hear from the other room. (In further experiments in which the learner was in the same room with them, the subjects could also see his tortured appearance.)

Contrary to predictions, most subjects continued to administer the electric shock right up to the supposed limit of 450 volts, labeled "Danger: Severe Shock." When the learner was in the same room 40 percent of the subjects continued to the end of the scale and even when the subject was required to force the learner's hand down onto the shock plate and hold it there against his struggles, 30 percent applied the most severe shocks possible. To appreciate these results it is important to understand that the acting of the learner was very convincing; follow-up studies confirmed that almost all the subjects believed that shocks were actually being administered and that the man was suffering severe pain.

Many of the subjects showed evidence of great stress as they complied with the experimenter's instructions. What direct pressure made the subjects continue despite their own distress at what they were doing? It consisted of the following statements, said firmly but politely by the experimenter, using as many of them as might be needed to overcome the subject's protests and concerns:

"Please continue, [or] please go on," "The experiment requires that you continue," "It is absolutely essential that you continue," "You have no other choice, you *must* go on." There were no threats, no physical coercion, no other inducements.

Milgram came to the conclusion that in such situations people enter into what he terms an *agentic state*, one in which they see themselves as agents for carrying out another person's wishes. This shift from autonomous functioning to submission to a hierarchy of command is considered by Milgram to be an evolutionary development that has enabled human beings to take advantage of the benefits of being in large groups. Unfortunately, it may also lead one to administer suffering on others if it is justified by authority.[39]

> The human element behind the agencies and institutions is denied. Thus, when the experimenter says, "The experiment *requires* that you continue," the subject feels this to be an imperative that goes beyond any merely human command. He does not ask the seemingly obvious question, "Whose experiment? Why should the designer be served while the victim suffers?" The wishes of a man—the designer of the experiment—have become part of a schema which exerts on the subject's mind a force that transcends the personal.[40]

It is easy to see how this type of justification has led to nations' transgressing human values. In our own country after the Japanese bombed Pearl Harbor, blameless American citizens were dispossessed and forcibly moved into internment camps for the duration of the war because they were of Japanese descent. In the name of national security the fundamental values and principles of our democracy were thrust aside and great injustice done. Similarly, as a nation (and despite internal dissent), we justified our actions in Vietnam by the concept of "fighting Communist aggression" as we attempted to defoliate the forests with Agent Orange and napalmed civilians. The American government has supported—and still supports—governments whose murderous savagery and sickening use of torture equals, if not surpasses, Stalin's and, with the possible exception of genocide, rivals that of the Nazis. We are likely to be told that the national interest requires our support. Just as the experiment in Milgram's study assumed an impersonal, overriding authority, even more so does the national interest. As Noam Chomsky noted in a symposium on human rights:

> The concept of "national interest" [is] a mystification that serves to conceal the ways in which state policy is formed and executed . . . Within a particular nation-state, some groups are sufficiently powerful to exert a major, perhaps dominant, influence over state policy and the ideological systems. Their special interests then become, in effect, "the national interest." To take again the case of Guatemala: in 1954 the United Fruit Company had an interest in blocking land reform: I did not . . . What was "the national interest"? In practice, it was the special interest of those with the power to influence and execute state policy and to shape the basic structure of the ideological system, including the flow of information.[41]

We can understand the power of "the experiment," "the state," and "the national interest" if we recognize these abstractions as representing Higher Authority: the parent of the dependency fantasy who protects, rewards, and punishes.

Appreciation of the power and ubiquitous nature of the dependency fantasy helps us to understand how, at every level of government and society, people set aside any doubts by assuming that "they" must know what they are doing. Often, "they" are not to be found. Even national leaders can react like small children ready to believe that the driver of the car must be wise. But the "shepherds" are not different from the "sheep."

Devaluing the Outsider

THE security of a cult is bound up with the idea of being special, better than those outside the group. Indeed, outsiders are likely to be seen as threatening since they do not share the cult's belief in the leader and in the special entitlement of its members. This threat is met by devaluing the non-believers. In part, this devaluation is an expression of the child's wish that his or her parents be the most powerful, that they know everything and can obtain for their children good things which others do not have. Furthermore, feeling blessed and favored confers a sense of protection, calming anxieties about the world outside.

Devaluing the outsider is probably the most common cult-like behavior in everyday society, where it takes the form of regarding one's opponents as if they were a homogeneous group with only negative traits. Bad motives are attributed to the other, but not to oneself. This devaluation is usually done by designating the adversary as, for example, "stupid," "rigid," "lazy," "reactionary," "bleeding heart," "cold." When one devalues another no real proof is offered. There is seldom any inquiry into the actual statements and actions of members of the "bad" group, or any serious consideration of the adversary's point of view and its possible validity, and critical analysis of one's own "good" view, discriminating between assumptions and facts, rarely takes place.

Examples of this everyday cult behavior can be found on radio talk shows. One major program I have encountered has a host who is perpetually exclaiming at the stupidity of whatever political or bureaucratic figure is the target for the day. He and the caller-in indulge in a festival of indignation and self-congratulation, shaking their collective heads over the "ridiculous" actions that have so astonished them, seldom seeking to understand how the action under attack might be reasonable from a different point of view or even being genuinely curious about it. Instead, the host and the caller engage in cult behavior. By designating someone else as bad or stupid, they are reassured that they themselves are good, their views commendable.

.   .   .

Perhaps the most important thing to understand about devaluing the outsider is that it is a necessary preliminary to harming others, to doing violence. Whether the conflict is between nations or individuals, the attacker devalues the victim prior to the violent act. Sociologist Jack Katz studied street gangs and juvenile delinquents and noted the special function of cursing in propelling an attack.

> Cursing . . . is a direct and effective way of doing just what it appears to do: symbolically transforming the offending party into an ontologically lower status . . . If the other is a shit, attacking him becomes a community service—a form of moral garbage collection performed on behalf of all decent people . . . Cursing at once makes the accursed repulsive and conjures up an altruistic overlay for an attack on him or her.[1]

The person you devalue becomes easier to kill. But when you look at him, be sure you do not see who he really is, for if you do, you cannot believe he is inferior to you. A man who had been a medical corpsman in Vietnam remembers the time when he was asked to guard an old Viet Cong. His prisoner looked right into his eyes, and the corpsman looked back. Then the old man was dragged to death behind a truck.

> I will never forget the man's face, and I will never forget his eyes, and I will never forget holding the rifle at his face . . . I'll

never forget how old he was. There was something about the internal solidity of this human being that I will never forget . . . Something went on that changed my life.[2]

Devaluation relies heavily on projection, "a defense mechanism, operating unconsciously, in which what is emotionally unacceptable in the self is unconsciously rejected and attributed (projected) to others."[3] Projection occurs when we attribute to others those aspects of ourselves that we wish to deny. By identifying the bad impulse or trait as being outside ourselves, we can feel more secure. Thus, projection offers protection from the anxiety of being bad and the punishment of being abandoned. In addition, by making other people bad in our own mind, we can legitimize behavior toward them that would otherwise be morally unacceptable, even to the point of sanctioning cruel and vicious actions.

I saw a vivid demonstration of projection at the conclusion of a five-day group relations conference when I joined a small group that was discussing what had been learned. Opposite me was a stocky, muscular young man with a hostile demeanor. I felt that he would physically attack me if I gave him the slightest excuse. I was afraid of him. My feelings were similar to what I had felt toward school bullies when I was growing up. Because during the conference we had dealt with projection, I tried questioning myself to see if I had any aggressive impulses toward the man whom I was afraid of. Immediately, I became aware of a desire to attack, to punch him to the ground. The violence in me was unmistakable. I looked again at the young man and could not believe the transformation that had taken place. He now appeared mild, nonthreatening, a perfectly nice person. This reversal of perception had happened in that instant of recognition of my own hostile feelings. The experience was vivid, probably because the conference had been designed to intensify projective defenses, but I am sure that similar distortions of perception take place under more normal conditions and that these perceptions can also be reversed.

The effect of projection is often a perception of the other person as being fundamentally different, a morally inferior species, undeserving of empathy. Perhaps the most common form of projection is to condemn others without noting good qualities that may lessen our sense of distance between them and us. In fact, noting an enemy's less admirable similarities to us can provoke strong feelings. Many people were distressed when Hannah Arendt's study of Adolph Eichmann, the Nazi war criminal, led her to conclude that he was not diabolical, but banal, a poor thinker, common.[4] Although the research of Stanley Milgram[5] and Philip Zimbardo[6] suggests strongly that the potential for cruelty and the carrying out of heinous orders is common to all human beings, it is hard for us to acknowledge that we may be less unlike the Nazis than we would wish. Projection protects us all from what we fear.

The more authoritarian the human social system, the more likely a separatist world view will arise because any anger or resentment stimulated in the follower by his or her submission to the leader requires displacement onto other persons—the outsider, the infidel, the non-believer. Feelings of rebellion toward the leader, which are defined by the group as evil, make the cult member anxious, even ready to believe in satanic possession, an apt metaphor to describe the sensation of being invaded by unwanted feelings and images. Projection and a division of humanity into the saved and the damned are called into play with increasing intensity. As a result, the more rigid the system the more powerful is the belief in the Devil or Evil—and the more violent the feelings toward the outsider.

Because projection requires the establishment of separation, of discontinuity, of fundamental differences, the person or group onto whom the badness is projected must be a "not-me"; otherwise one's condemnation would rebound onto oneself. For this reason we project most often onto other nations, other racial and religious groups, opposing political parties, and economic and social classes different from our own. However, projection may also be used in ordinary social relationships when the need to feel superior rather than inferior arises often.

Thus, we increase our moral security by seeing others as evil, stupid, backward, or arrogant. When we do this we create and maintain cult consciousness in a fashion similar to the fanatic who perceives outsiders as damned, degenerate, and suitable for killing. When average, non-fanatic citizens devalue others they rarely murder them as a consequence, but they may well acquiesce in a political order that does.

Upon reflection you can probably identify your own focus of projection, your "not-me": Republicans, Democrats, rich, poor, black, white, Christian, Jew, Muslim, Northerner, Southerner, dove, hawk, old, young, men, women. Projection is so much a part of our thinking we seldom notice it, except when someone else does it. Again, I heard a radio talk show provide a fine example when a caller made the following comment about a political candidate: "I wouldn't vote for him; he's a Southerner. They're all prejudiced."

· · ·

One of the symptoms of projection is an attitude of righteousness coloring persons' statements of their beliefs and views of others. As we have seen, through projection we reassure ourselves that we are good (as in the child's world) by pointing out that someone else is bad. The covert "I am good" is signalled by self-righteousness, which requires the devaluation of someone else.

Self-righteousness is the dominant attitude of cult members, although it may be masked by false humility and public confessions of unworthiness. Righteousness has a special vocabulary that establishes two species of human beings. Jerry Falwell put it clearly: "The war is not between fundamentalists and liberals but between those who love Jesus Christ and those who hate him."[7]

Of course, the vocabulary of righteousness is seldom as stark outside of the religious or political arenas, but may include such terms as "unscientific," "neurotic," and "infantile," as opposed to "mature," "realistic," and "rigorous." Being thus negatively labeled amounts to rejection. Understandably, we are usually very sensitive to our own group's criteria for inclusion or casting-out.

Righteousness protects against self-doubt and at the same time provides a rationale for actions that would otherwise place us in the bad category. By intensifying righteousness a person can retain the feeling of being good while performing shameful acts; cruelty is justified, may even become a duty. The breaking of Clara's ties with her child, the splitting of couples, and the alienation of Hugh from his dying brother were all supposedly done for the highest spiritual reasons, as sacrifices for the high purposes of the group.

The following example of righteousness running amok is from a speech by the late Ayatollah Khomeini, who established a theocracy in Iran:

If one permits an infidel to continue in his role as a corrupter of the earth, his moral suffering will be all the worse. If one kills the infidel, and thus stops him from perpetrating his misdeeds, his death will be a blessing to him. For if he remains alive, he will become more and more corrupt. This is a surgical operation commanded by God the all-powerful.

. . . Those who have knowledge of the suffering in the life to come realize that cutting off the hand of someone for a crime he has committed is of benefit to him. In the Beyond he will thank those who, on earth, executed the will of God.[8]

There is no cruelty like the cruelty of the righteous.

Righteousness can be seen in many one would assume were not susceptible to cult thinking, scientists, for example. Proponents of theories which challenge accepted views are sometimes vilified with a zeal that combines righteousness and arrogance. One example from the history of medicine is that of the nineteenth-century Hungarian physician, I. P. Semmelweis. Semmelweis came to the conclusion that the high incidence of puerperal fever (which killed many in childbirth) among women who delivered their babies in hospitals was due to contamination by attending physicians who, at that time, routinely went from the autopsy room to the delivery room without cleansing their hands. His theory and his recommendation that physicians wash was received with such ridicule and followed by such professional persecution that he eventually went mad.

A more current example of the effects of scientific righteousness and the arrogance it fosters is provided by the development of the atomic bomb. Although the research was initially justified by the fear that the Nazis would attain the bomb first, the work did not stop when that concern was eliminated by the Allied invasion of Europe. Only one scientist left the enterprise; the rest continued what they had begun. Recently we have begun to recognize the responsibility borne by scientists for the nuclear threat that now hangs over the world. Following a reunion at Los Alamos of many who had worked on the atomic bomb, Isador Rabi, the Nobel prize–winning physicist, was asked if he thought it likely that there would ever again be such a collection of scientists working with the same dedication and idealism. "Rabi's response was unhesitating. 'I hope not,' he said. 'We had no doubts about what we were doing.'"[9]

． ． ．

Religions are particularly prone to devaluing outsiders because to accord outsiders equal status is to give respectability to their different versions of God and lessen the certainty of faith. Doubt may arise.

Even if the outsider is not specifically devalued, scorned, or hated, theistic religions tend to reward followers with special status: the Jews are the chosen, good Christians are saved from hell, true Muslims go to paradise. The non-believer, in many instances, is a damned infidel. Within religions different sects or denominations vary in the absoluteness of this judgment, but the basic attitude is often the same—else why profess that faith over some other? Because my faith is true! a devout believer may exclaim.

But it is not the search for truth which leads a person to massacre or torture, to ostracize and expel, to scorn and to hate; nor is it a search for bliss or other, spiritual, states. In subtle or not so subtle ways, most religions utilize devaluation despite their best intentions. If you think not, listen closely to the next sermon you hear.

The consequences for the outsider can be significant indeed. Because religions deal in absolutes, the devaluation of the outsider can be absolute also, justifying behavior toward the innocent and helpless which the religion's founder would have condemned and which by any humane standard is barbaric. The Crusades were often a license for the murder, rape, and devastation of "infidel" peoples, those with different religious beliefs. Within Christianity, the religious passions of Catholics and Protestants fueled the Thirty Years' War which almost totally destroyed Germany in the seventeenth century. More recently, Hindus and Moslems created the nightmare of fighting in Bangladesh, featuring indiscriminate slaughter and numerous examples of gang rape all under the banner of their respective religions.

Less violent forms of devaluation are almost universal. Members of most religions can be hostile, or at best uneasy, at the prospect of their children marrying outside the faith, even outside the particular sect to which they belong. When a son or daughter of Orthodox Jewish parents marries a non-Jew the parents sometimes conduct services for the dead, psychologically burying their errant child. Until 1984, a non-Catholic who married a Catholic had to sign a promise to raise their children as Catholics if the couple were to be married by a priest.

This exclusivity is not hard to understand. All groups exist by virtue of membership boundaries; the more lax those boundaries the weaker is group cohesion and group strength. As a consequence, group boundaries are defended vigorously. Since intermarriage poses the greatest danger to religious boundaries, it is punished in overt or subtle ways; natural family ties may be subordinated to the larger religious group. As in extreme cults, family bonds may be seen as secondary to preserving the exclusiveness of the religion, the superior status of the followers and the inferior status of those outside.

Fundamentalist religions, in particular, tend to devalue the outsider to preserve the certainty of their scriptures and their leader's connection with God. In recent years, a conservative American Christian fundamentalism has experienced a resurgence and now claims many millions of members. (Since many of these fundamentalists are also members of mainline churches, it is hard to know exactly how large the group is, but informed estimates suggest they number well over twenty million.)[10] Over recent years this movement has established powerful radio and television broadcasting networks, made extensive use of direct mail for fundraising and recruitment, and sponsored a vast increase in fundamentalist parochial schools where authoritarian, separatist, sectarian views are taught. Many teach that only "true" Christians—those "born again"—will be saved; the rest will go to hell. The Jim Bakker and Jimmy Swaggart scandals did not appreciably change the popularity of these religious movements.

As evil and an assortment of devils came to dominate the consciousness of Alex Monroe and the Life Force group, Satan and evil spirits dominate the world of many fundamentalist religious sects, whether Christian, Islamic or of any other denomination.

•   •   •

Even in psychiatry, the readiness to classify as alien those who do not belong to one's group may result in a devaluation similar in kind to that which what takes place in cults. This is not usually identified as cult behavior because there is no specific cult of psychiatry nor, with few exceptions, are there hospital cult leaders. Nevertheless, the use of projection may occur and the result is a distortion of reality and adverse effects on the "outsider."

To identify with a person who is crying because his or her spouse has left is not difficult for a psychiatrist. To identify with one who is screaming, smearing feces, psychotically suicidal, assaultive, or self-mutilating is quite another matter. Although the impulses represented by extreme, psychotic behaviors are present to some degree in every person, including the psychiatrist, they constitute precisely those impulses most strenuously suppressed and rigidly controlled. The deepest infantile wishes are represented in the overt and seemingly guilt-free regression of psychotic patients, who abandon the status of the adult for the humiliation and gratifications of the infant. Such passive, infantile wishes are more taboo in our culture than neurotic sexual behavior. I believe the difference in treatment usually given people exhibiting psychotic symptoms versus the treatment provided for those whose symptoms are closer to the therapist's cannot be understood only as the result of a belief in biochemical causation of psychosis. Rather, I think we need to recognize a therapist's unconscious wish to see as alien the person whose behavior represents the bad qualities that threaten rejection in one's own group.

I believe this separation and devaluation lies behind the striking difference one can observe between the way psychiatric treatment is conducted in outpatient departments and the way treatment is provided to inpatients, even in university-affiliated hospitals. Inpatients receive drug therapy with neuroleptic drugs such as Thorazine or Haldol, plus a smattering of psychological treatment under the euphemism of supportive therapy. If psychiatric residents are being trained on the ward, patients may also have individual psychotherapy, but neither patient nor novice therapist expect it to be effective (and under these conditions psychotherapy seldom is). In contrast, most outpatients receive analytically oriented psychotherapy, psychological treatment based on psychodynamic principles, unless the outpatient is a transfer from the hospital; in that case, therapy is often focused on medication, dealing with drug side-effects, and managing the living situation. (Such patients are often seen for less than the fifty-minute hour usual for outpatient therapy.)

The division of patients into two classes, the psychotherapy-outpatient group and the medication-inpatient group, seldom receives critical comment, nor does the fact that inpatient procedures frequently violate the psychodynamic principles assumed to be operative for outpatients. For example, at one medical school where I taught, nursing students were assigned young, first-time schizophrenic patients with whom they were expected to establish rapport and a therapeutic relationship. After six weeks the nursing students left for other duties; psychiatric residents stayed for six months, then they too left. These practices were standard despite the knowledge that the loss of a parent, spouse, or lover was often the precipitating event for the psychosis from which the patient was suffering. The departures of the nursing students and the residents could only intensify feelings of loss. One had to conclude that psychodynamic considerations received short shrift on the hospital ward.

Another indicator of the separate status of inpatients at this hospital was that although medication was supposed to be individually prescribed, almost everyone admitted to the unit with a diagnosis of schizophrenia arrived from the emergency room heavily dosed with neuroleptic drugs, and on the ward, the neuroleptics were continued. As a result, no drug-free period of observation and treatment planning occurred. If behavior did not improve, the drug dosage was increased.

When we studied the exact sequence of events that preceded a decision by ward staff to increase a patient's medication, we found that in almost every case the patient had shifted from inactivity, depression, or apathy to being noisy, "crazy," threatening, or messy. The possibility that this shift might signify progress in the patient, a beginning attempt to communicate feelings, was not considered. Where exploration, uncovering, and communication were highly valued in outpatient services, in the inpatient world management and suppression of behavior had priority.

The dividing line between neurotic (outpatient) and psychotic (inpatient) problems is not completely clear; it appears to be only if one compares the most healthy neurotic patients and the most psychotic. So many people suffer from intermediate conditions that the diagnosis of "borderline" has had to be employed as a bridging category. Even the diagnosis of schizophrenia encompasses such a wide variety of conditions that numerous sub-types are employed and the diagnostic criteria are non-specific and constantly revised. If one grants that both environmental (psychological) and biochemical factors influence human behavior, the sharp split in psychiatric practice cannot be defended on rational grounds.

The split occurs, I believe, partly because the seriously disturbed patient is devalued as an outsider by the psychiatrist. This became clear when a colleague and I changed a drug-oriented psychiatric ward into an intensive psychological treatment unit, one that focused on the relation between early life experience and the patient's behavior on the ward.[11] Drugs were not used unless psychological treatment proved ineffective. As a result of this change in orientation, staff paid much more attention to the ward dynamics and the role of both patients and staff in intensifying or diminishing psychotic behavior. There was much to learn.

One day "Jerry," a weird-looking adolescent sitting crouched in a wheelchair and diagnosed as paranoid and retarded, was admitted (by mistake) to our ward instead of being shipped off to the state hospital for what I would call warehousing. Jerry seemed like an idiot, would occasionally drool, liked to wheel rapidly around the ward with a crazy look on his face, and replied to questions and orders only in the most halting manner. The nurses were afraid of him, but we had to keep him for a few days until a transfer could be arranged. During this time one of the nurses remarked that she didn't think Jerry was as retarded as he seemed; she thought he knew what he was doing. So we confronted him, saying, "Jerry, what's this big act you've got, trying to scare everyone? You're not that crazy, you're not that dumb."

A big smile spread slowly over his face and the crazy look went away. We never did send him to the state hospital. He wasn't an idiot. He was paranoid, but not severely, and much of his behavior related to family dynamics which then became the focus of treatment. Jerry was more like us than different, doing what he thought necessary to meet his needs and protect himself. He had made use of people's readiness to see him as alien, to devalue him, in order to gain power for himself, the power of frightening others and of being able to hide.

"Juanita," a very depressed Mexican–Indian woman in late middle age who had almost no formal education and spoke very little English showed us how outsider status can be conveyed by cultural differences as well as by psychiatric symptoms. Juanita gave all the appearance of a backward peasant who could not comprehend much of what was going on around her. We gave her a suitable therapeutic task for someone as limited as she seemed to be—cleaning tables. Before long, Juanita was causing considerable turmoil on the ward, covertly expressing her anger at the staff and other patients. We were forced to recognize that underneath, Juanita was a strategic planner like the rest of us. When we were able to see who Juanita was, we took her off the cleaning job and treated her as a conscious, equal member of the patient group. Her depression decreased and the disturbance on the ward disappeared.

■   ■   ■

Media owners, editors, and reporters, like other people, are motivated by ideals, not just money or power. Most believe (some passionately) that reporting the society's imperfections and providing the public with a diversity of views and information is their special function and responsibility, that which gives meaning to their work. (I am speaking here of societies which value a free press.) The problem is that discharging that responsibility may conflict with support for the status quo. One way in which this dilemma can be solved is by being careful to report that dissent exists while devaluing it at the same time. This can be done covertly, even unconsciously, by means of the selected image.

Most newsmagazines and newspapers maintain a file of photos of prominent people and it is easy to select one in which a politician or other celebrity looks ridiculous, sinister, or ugly. Additionally, the photo can be juxtaposed with one that flatters whomever the editor wishes to promote. If you look for this device you will see it used frequently, especially at election time. Technically, it is fair, all sides are receiving publicity.

The selected image is used most powerfully by television, which presents, after all, a series of discrete scenes while attempting to convey a reality much larger than what can be framed. What the commentator or editor selects tells a part of the story, not the whole story. The power of the selected image resides in the fact that we respond to newsphotos and television as if they are showing us objective facts devoid of interpretation. The image seems to validate itself. Sociologist Todd Gitlin experienced this aspect of the media as a leader of Students for a Democratic Society (SDS). Later, he analyzed the media's use of the image and found that

> news photos operate under a hidden sign marked, "this really happened, see for yourself." Of course, the choice of *this* moment of an event as against that, of *this* person rather than that, of *this* angle rather than any other, indeed, the selection of this photographed incident to represent a whole complex chain of events and meanings, is a highly ideological procedure. But, by appearing literally to reproduce the event as it *really* happened, news photos suppress their selective/interpretive/ideological function. They seek a warrant in that ever pre-given, neutral structure, which is beyond question, beyond interpretation: the "real world."[12]

Television makes optimum use of this see-for-yourself power. Consequently, in many parts of the world, the nightly news shows probably shape people's perception of events more vividly and more effectively than any other source of information. Considering this power, it is worth noting that what appears on the ABC, CBS, and NBC nightly newscasts is a selection and interpretation largely created by six people, the executive producers and anchorpersons of each of the three networks.

Words also can be used very effectively to devalue opposition. I remember how the media in the early sixties characterized the members of SANE (myself being one of them) who opposed the atmospheric testing of nuclear weapons. While dutifully reporting our campaign, the media tended to dismiss us as having no significance; one columnist called us "small dogs barking at an express train." Being consigned to ineffective canine status was a frustrating and depressing experience. The media preferred the image of President Kennedy, who dramatically drank a glass of milk at a convention of dairy farmers to express his disdain for charges by SANE that nuclear testing was contaminating milk products with strontium 90. Fortunately, the media were wrong. After Kennedy eventually signed a treaty banning atmospheric testing, SANE acquired respect.

The same devaluing, followed eventually by acceptance, has taken place with regard to anti–nuclear power activists. The accidents at Three Mile Island and, later, Chernobyl resulted in the anti-nuclear movement being legitimized; groups that had been ridiculed now receive more serious treatment than in the past. However, those who challenge nuclear weapons development by committing civil disobedience at Lawrence Livermore Laboratories or at submarine bases and missile sites are still labeled radical. Their arrest by police is reported, but their critique of weapons policy rarely is.

Reality may be distorted simply by screening out dissenting views without the outright censorship seen in totalitarian countries; reality may be distorted by giving great prominence and validity to the established view while devaluing dissenters and making them marginal. Gay rights activists, anti-nuclear groups, and others outside the establishment evoke clear contemporary examples of devaluation. The treatment of student dissidents in the mainstream media during the 1960s offers good examples of the use of negative adjectives and selective photos combined with the ignoring or minimizing of the issues raised. As Gitlin pointed out with regard to American politics of the sixties, an official typically was given the voice of calm rationality; dissidents were often portrayed as unreasonable, naive, impulsive, ridiculous, violent and extreme. Some may have been, to be sure, but those who were not were seldom given a forum.

> Most of the time the taken-for-granted code of "objectivity" and "balance" presses reporters to seek out scruffy-looking, chanting, "Viet Cong" flag-waving demonstrators and to counterpose them to reasonable-sounding, fact-brandishing authorities . . . Hotheads carry on, the message connotes, while wiser heads, officials and reporters both, with superb self-control, watch the unenlightened ones make trouble.[13]

Writing about the same era, Daniel Hallin found a similar devaluation in the media, in which protest was equated with violence, authority with competence and order.

> Cronkite began one report on college antiwar protests by saying, "The Cambodia development set off a new round of antiwar demonstrations on U.S. campuses, and not all of them were peaceful." The film report, not surprisingly, was about one of the ones that was *not* peaceful, and dealt mainly with

the professionalism shown by the authorities who restored order.[14]

In contrast, when the protest occurs in a communist country, American news media are likely to handle it differently. During the June 1989 demonstrations in Tiananmen Square, in China's capital, the students were presented in a sympathetic light; their point of view and statements by their representatives were carried by all the American media.

Of course, devaluation also takes place in the American media's coverage of international affairs. Consider the view of the Soviet Union that was maintained by our mainstream media until very recently. Princeton University professor Stephen Cohen describes

> a pattern of media coverage that systematically highlights the negative aspects of the Soviet domestic system while obscuring the positive ones. Soviet crop failures and abuses of political liberties have been the regular focus of American news stories since the early 1970s, but expanded welfare programs and the rising living standard have gone largely unreported . . .
>
> Much American commentary on Soviet affairs employs special political terms that are inherently biased and laden with double standards . . . The United States has a government, security organizations and allies. The Soviet Union, however, has a regime, secret police and satellites. Our leaders are consummate politicians; theirs are wily, cunning or worse. We give the world information and seek influence; they disseminate propaganda and disinformation while seeking expansion and domination.[15]

Following Gorbachev's announcement of the policy of *glasnost* and his visit to the United States, a marked change has taken place in media coverage of the Soviet Union. For the first time that I can remember, television has shown me Russians in surroundings much like mine, enjoying themselves, voicing concerns for country, children, peace—Russians *like us*. According to my TV set, Russia has undergone a chromatic revolution, as well. Where before it had been grey, now it is in color. The weather has also changed. Sunshine has occurred in Russian cities for the first time in 40 years.

There is an implicit devaluation of others in nationalism. I consider myself to be internationally minded, free of jingoism. However, not long ago, curious to hear what other countries were saying about world events, I bought a shortwave radio. As I dialed from one foreign station to another, I was surprised to find that the United States was not the center of the world. In Brazil, South American affairs and not those of the United States were being discussed; in England, the focus was local politics and reactions to a proposed tunnel to France. The effect was a little eerie; my own country seemed to have disappeared. I knew that nationalism was a pervasive phenomenon, but my own parochialism—revealed by my surprise—had been unrecognized.

■ ■ ■

Devaluation of other nations seen as enemies is a pervasive problem for governments. An example from the era of the cold war of our own negative stereotyping is the general surprise and consternation that occurred when the USSR launched Sputnik, the first satellite. Soviets, who were regarded as backward, primitive totalitarians, weren't supposed to be able to do this. Truman is said to have expressed his own surprise that "those Asiatics" could do something like that.[16] Similar surprise greeted the first test of a hydrogen bomb by the USSR.[17]

Misperception of the enemy (basically a devaluing of the foreigner), seeing its people as less advanced, less principled, less admirable, and more deserving of punishment and harsh treatment than ourselves, has affected international relations throughout history, contributing to conflict and to spirals of increased armaments. The arms race is not a new phenomenon and the view that the enemy must be "dealt with firmly" has had adherents. Political scientist Robert Jervis, in discussing the way misperception takes place in international relations, cites two statesmen of the nineteenth century, whose devaluing statements mirror each other:

[James Polk:] . . . if Congress faultered [sic] or hesitated in their course, John Bull would immediately become arrogant and more grasping in his demands; & that such had been the history of the Brittish [sic] Nation in all their contests with other Powers for the last two hundred years.[18]

[Lord Palmerston:] A quarrel with the United States is . . . undesirable . . . [but] in dealing with Vulgar minded Bullies, and such unfortunately the people of the United States are, nothing is gained by submission to Insult & wrong; on the contrary the submission to an Outrage only encourages the commission of another and a greater one—such people are always trying how far they can venture to go; and they generally pull up when they find they can go no further without encountering resistance of a formidable Character.[19]

Polk was ready to see Britain as responding only to "firmness," meaning force, while Palmerston had the same view of the United States. Each was the outsider to the other and, accordingly, was devalued to maintain the righteousness and purity of the home nation's position, as in the following (one of countless modern examples of reciprocal devaluation):

[John Foster Dulles:] Khrushchev does not need to be convinced of our good intentions. He knows we are not aggressors and do not threaten the security of the Soviet Union.[20]

[Khrushchev:] It is quite well known that if one tries to appease a bandit by first giving him one's purse, then one's coat, and so forth, he is not going to be more charitable because of this, he is not going to stop exercising his banditry. On the contrary, he will become ever more insolent.[21]

The righteous indignation of contemporary leaders echoes statesmen throughout history who have believed that the armaments of others demonstrate aggressive intentions but did not apply that reasoning to arms build-ups of their own. Estimation of the significance of another country's military budget is especially vulnerable to this error. Intra-service rivalries and parochial political maneuvering are at least as important in promoting the current arms race as any grand, organized strategy, but neither the USSR nor the United States appear to give these factors much weight in evaluating the armaments decisions of the other side, certainly not as far as public pronouncements are concerned.[22] The psychological problem is that recognizing these internal con-

cerns would soften the distinction between good and evil governments and suggest areas of uncomfortable similarity.

Devaluation of the enemy played a role in the Bay of Pigs disaster. Journalist Peter H. Wyden believes it was a pivotal
factor,

> The final arrogance, the failure to inform themselves about
> Castro's strength and his people's spirit or even to inform their
> own infiltration teams, I attribute to the gook syndrome.
> American policy-makers suffer from it chronically. They tend
> to underestimate grossly the capabilities and determination of
> people who committed the sin of not having been born Amer-
> icans, especially "gooks" whose skins are less than white.[23]

The same devaluation, leading to far more tragic blunders,
took place later in Southeast Asia. Shad Meshad, who had been a
psychology officer in Vietnam, recalls his attitude:

> I was from the southeastern part of the United States, and
> spent my entire life there . . . I knew nothing about Asians.
> The only thing I did know about them were the names we
> gave them, both four-letter words, "gook" and "dink." And
> our attitude was that the only good dink is a dead dink. This
> was my introduction to the culture of Asia.[24]

Devaluing the outsider is made manifest in righteousness, in
blindness to the implications of one's own behavior, in the refusal
to acknowledge similar intentions on both sides, in the identification of the other as bad in contrast to oneself as good. All these
are hallmarks of cult behavior. While examples of this abound on
both sides of the iron curtain, Ronald Reagan provided a prime
specimen in his "evil empire" speech.

> Let us be aware that while they [the Soviet Union] preach the
> supremacy of the state, declare its omnipotence over individ-
> ual man, and predict its eventual domination of all peoples on
> the Earth—they are the focus of evil in the modern world . . .
> I urge you to beware the temptation of pride—the temptation
> of blithely declaring yourselves above it all and label both sides
> equally at fault, to ignore the facts of history and the aggres-
> sive impulses of an evil empire, to simply call the arms race a
> giant misunderstanding and thereby remove yourself from the
> struggle between right and wrong and good and evil.[25]

Certainly when one considers Stalin's starvation of the kulaks, the monstrous gulag prison system, or the barbarities the Soviets have committed in Afghanistan, there is justification for the use of the term evil. Reagan's speech, however, showed no awareness of moral lapses of our own which, although markedly different in degree, are not so totally different in kind as to justify the self-righteousness of his pronouncement.

Unwillingness to acknowledge one's own evil is characteristic of all government leaders. It is precisely that need for purity of self-image, for displacement of all badness onto the enemy, that is "the temptation of pride" of which Reagan spoke, but did not apply to himself. In that same speech, in complete innocence of the image's applicability to himself, he cited C. S. Lewis:

"The greatest evil is not done now in those sordid 'dens of crime' that Dickens loved to paint. It is not even done in concentration camps and labor camps. In those we see its final result. But it is conceived and ordered (moved, seconded, carried, and minuted) in clean, carpeted, warmed, and well-lighted offices, by quiet men with white collars and cut fingernails and smooth-shaven cheeks who do not need to raise their voice." [26]

■ ■ ■

In every person's life, given a psychologically threatening situation, devaluation can extend to friends with the consequence that slights and insults may be perceived when none are intended. I remember hearing Abraham Maslow, the psychologist who helped create humanistic psychology, as he reminisced about his life and spoke of his sense that his own death was near. Shortly before, he had made a pilgrimage across the United States to visit all the people with whom he had once been friends but had fallen out. He wanted to understand what had happened. What he learned was sad, ironic, and hopeful at the same time. In each case he and the friend had had an interaction whose meaning was ambiguous; Maslow might have ignored an invitation or the other person might have behaved coldly toward him. Of all the possible explanations that he or his friend considered at the time—he's worried about his job, he forgot, he is ill, he's angry at me, he dislikes me—each placed at the top of the list the explanation that was least flattering to himself. And in every case they were wrong.

I call this the Maslow principle and frequently tell the story to my patients, since the problem comes up so often. Even in daily life, it is often hard to realize that the other person is just like us, to see him or her at eye level. Almost everyone tends to give a negative interpretation to another person's behavior in ambiguous situations. When we do this, it seems logical; when someone else does it, we find it paranoid and hard to believe.

Governments, composed of people, behave no differently. As Jervis points out, they usually view the actions of other governments as deliberate and give scant consideration to the possibility that confusion, chaos, accidents, and coincidence may be responsible; that the consequences of the other's actions may have been unintended.

Although stupidity and confusion may be responsible for a particular government action (these factors operate at least as frequently as cunning and deceit), they are seldom given much weight when analyzing the actions of an opposing country. When the German battleship *Goeben* escaped from a superior British force at the beginning of World War I, the Germans tried to understand why the escape had been possible. "To attribute this *coup* to a blunder on the part of the British admiral in command seemed so unlikely that Bethmann-Hollweg and the German Chief of the Admiralty were inclined to conclude that Britain was unwilling to strike any 'heavy blows' against Germany."[27] The Germans ended up seriously miscalculating British intentions, with very adverse consequences for Germany.

Everyday paranoia can extend to the business world, where the battle is economic; cultural differences may be ignored in favor of explanations assuming craftiness or conspiracy. For example, discussions over the joint production of the Concorde almost broke down and aborted the project when the French preference for Cartesian precision ran up against British preference for cautious empiricism.

Unfortunately [this preference] tends to make the French suspect the British more often of duplicity than of simplicity . . . One British aircraft executive involved [in conversations with the French over the Concorde] was reported as having complained that: "The French always think we're being Machiavellian, when in fact we're just muddling through."[28]

.   .   .

Recently we have had a devastating illustration of the price of devaluing the outsider—the failure of our society to respond adequately to the AIDS epidemic. Randy Shilts, in his book *And The Band Played On*, chronicled the lost opportunities to control the disease, the needless deaths of thousands of people, and the even greater losses to come in future years as a consequence of this neglect.[29]

The reason for our failure is clear. From early on, when its effects first appeared as a high incidence of Kaposi's sarcoma, AIDS was regarded as a disease of homosexuals. To many in mainstream American society, homosexuals are outsiders, ridiculed, feared and often despised as alien. Because it was homosexuals who were dying, few people outside that group cared. Extreme fundamentalists regarded AIDS as God's punishment, and others felt it served "them" right.

In contrast, Legionnaires' disease had evoked an instant, fully mobilized response by health agencies, the government, and the media, even though it was a less deadly, less horrible killer than AIDS. In the first twelve months of the AIDS epidemic, the Center for Disease Control had spent $1 million compared to $9 million spent on Legionnaires' disease.

Newspapers paid little notice to the growing AIDS disaster until intravenous drug users were afflicted. Drug addicts, too, are outcasts, but they are heterosexual. The first coverage of the epidemic by the *Wall Street Journal* came in 1982 under the headline, "New, Often-Fatal Illness in Homosexuals Turns Up in Women, Heterosexual Males."

Shilts's chronology of the disease is a chilling portrayal of the effects that devaluing the outsider can have upon the outcast group and, eventually, upon those who cast them out as well. After four years, AIDS cases in the United States totaled 9,000 and of these 4,300 people had died. No massive response by the government or the media had yet taken place.

To appreciate the magnitude of these figures it should be recalled that Legionnaires' disease had claimed 29 lives, the poisoned Tylenol capsules had caused 7 deaths. Both of these crises elicited mobilization of all the resources the nation could muster and front-page, extensive coverage by the news media.

Not until the middle of the 1980s, when it became clear that AIDS could strike anyone, did the media give AIDS the full treatment and the government follow suit. Unfortunately, by then there were 12,000 cases, 6,000 people had died, and a virus whose latency can run eight years or more was lodged in tens of thousands who would yet fall ill. (As of February 1990, reported AIDS cases totaled 121,000, with 72,000 deaths.)

Shilts describes how in Washington, Arthur Bennet, an AIDS sufferer, stood in the rain with other protesters and gestured toward the White House, saying, "I think in the beginning of this whole syndrome, that they, over there, and a lot of other people said, 'Let the faggots die. They're expendable.' I wonder if it would have been 1,500 Boy Scouts, what would have been done."[30]

6

Avoiding Dissent

ALTHOUGH we all need dissent as a corrective, cults tend to punish it, to inhibit and stifle disagreement and criticism, to restrict access to information that would challenge group beliefs.

Cults employ a variety of means to exclude dissent. Mail may be monitored or withheld, only certain literature allowed, and discordant views may be labeled bad or satanic. In addition, members' attention is confined to a narrow field; if free time is spent studying and reciting dogma there is less danger that subversive information will be encountered or, if it is, that it will be thought about and its implications understood. Dogma itself may be simplified into slogans, rendering members' thinking even more primitive and further hampering critical thought. These means are enhanced by the punishment the group and leader mete out for challenging authority.

Such coercive forces create conflicts. The cult member wishes to continue riding in the back seat of the car, but at the same time his or her self-respect is threatened by compliance with censorship and subjection to rewards and punishments. So the inhibition of dissent may be pushed out of awareness, become unconscious. Conscious and unconscious suppression and restriction of dissent is perhaps the most characteristic feature of cult life; the more severe the restriction, the more control exercised by the group and the leader.

Cults further restrict dissent through decreased contact with non-members. Outsiders are likely to raise critical questions about the leader and the group's activities, thus weakening the group fantasy. In addition, as discussed earlier, outsiders are a threat because they may be sources of support, self-esteem, and comfort, offsetting the need for the group. Research suggests that the fewer social ties a cult convert had before joining, the more likely it was that he or she would remain in the organization.[1] When Hugh and Clara Robinson finally made their escape from Life Force, their contact with outsiders was crucial.

■   ■   ■

Avoidance of dissent is a prominent feature of normal society. We assume that in the United States our free press (including radio and television) voices all the dissent we would need. There is no government censorship; the First Amendment shields the media from interference. However, although America's mainstream media pride themselves on being independent, balanced, objective, in practice those characteristics are more limited than most, including media personnel, realize. Dissent is exercised within certain unspoken boundaries; beyond those limits it is avoided, downplayed, or ignored. Because the mass media are the major source of many kinds of information for the public at large, media behavior has farreaching effects. The media can create by what it presents.

Ben Bagdikian, dean of the Graduate School of Journalism at the University of California, Berkeley (and former reporter, journalist, and *Washington Post* editor), comments on two key findings of his research on the mass media:

> What the public learns is heavily weighted by what serves the economic and political interests of the corporations that own the media . . .
>
> The naivete of working journalists about the influence of owners on the news they publish is more widespread than even my thirty years as a reporter and editor had led me to believe.[2]

Although our media enjoy great freedom, they are in a dependent relationship to three types of authority: the corporate world that owns them, the advertisers that provide their revenues, and the government figures upon whom they rely for information. These dependency relationships involve both conscious and unconscious pressures that result in an inhibition of dissent not usually noticed by the public or by reporters and journalists themselves.

■   ■   ■

Most of the 25,000 media outlets are owned by fewer than thirty large corporations, and three corporations (ABC, CBS, and NBC) dominate television. The boards of directors controlling the corporations are composed of people who also serve on the boards of other corporations, many of them advertisers, forming an interlocking network. This concentration of media power in the hands of a relatively few big businesses and financial institutions makes it possible for these organizations to exert behind-the-scenes control over our access to information.[3]

Bagdikian's work offers suggestive instances of corporate control. One case involved the Tribune Company of Chicago, publishers of the *Chicago Tribune*. A member of its board of directors was also a director of Sears, Roebuck at the time the Federal Trade Commission accused Sears of dishonest sales promotion and advertising. The *Chicago Tribune* did not report this news at all even though Sears national headquarters are in Chicago and the accusation would undoubtably have been of interest to its readers.[4]

The *San Francisco Chronicle* noted a more recent example:

A reference to the General Electric Co., which owns NBC, was removed from a report on shoddy products that was televised Thursday by the network's "Today" program.

The report focused on a federal investigation of inferior bolts used by U.S. industries in products such as airline jets and missile silos.

It included a reference to a discovery by engineers at General Electric that one of every three bolts used in their jet engines is inferior.[5]

Bagdikian cites other instances of what appear to be outright censorship—books that aroused corporate displeasure being pulled before, during, or after publication. These include *Counter-*

Revolutionary Violence by Noam Chomsky, *Dupont: Behind the Nylon Curtain* by Gerard Zilg, *Countercoup: The Struggle for the Control of Iran* by Kermit Roosevelt, and *Corporate Murder* by Mark Dowie.[6]

Clearly books are published and documentaries aired which are critical of the corporate world; newspapers and newsmagazines publish exposés of business or government leaders. However, the potential for control exists and may be exercised in more subtle ways than cancelling a book. Certain ideas which serve advertisers and business may be cultivated and established as fact in the minds of the general public. One example is the general belief that unions have caused a drop in American productivity, whereas from 1981 to 1987, the productivity of U.S. manufacturing workers as a whole increased an average of 4 percent, while hourly wages increased only 0.8 percent.[7] Unions undoubtedly have their own illusions, but it is the corporate view that tends to be voiced in the media serving the majority of our citizens.

Nicholas Johnson, formerly an FCC commissioner for eleven years, put the problem most directly: "The First Amendment rights belong to the owners, and the owners can exercise those rights by hiring people who will hire journalists who don't rock the boat, who don't attack advertisers, who don't challenge the establishment."[8]

■   ■   ■

The mass media also do little to inform their audiences of the power of advertisers to control the ideological content of media entertainment and, on occasion, media commentary. As the major revenue source for television, radio, and newspapers, advertisers have considerable influence over what appears. Their financial leverage is huge; in 1981, media businesses earned $33 billion from advertisers compared to $7 billion from readers and viewers.[9] The one who pays the piper often calls the tune. The American public sees itself at least somewhat through the special vision of advertisers.

Effects of advertiser influence were suggested by research at the Annenberg School of Communication that showed the world portrayed by television to be quite unrealistic.

Despite the fact that nearly half of the national income goes to the top fifth of the real population, the myth of [the] middle class as the all-American norm dominates the world of television . . . Blue-collar and service work occupies 67 percent of all Americans but only 10 percent of television characters . . . [On TV] men outnumber women at least three to one . . . older people (over 65) [comprise] one-fifth of their true proportion in the population . . .[10]

The prime American consumer is between eighteen and forty-nine years of age, white, upwardly mobile, and middle- or upper-middle-class and this is the group advertisers are most interested in reaching. The effect on the media audience is significant; viewers of low socioeconomic status who watch TV four or more hours per day are more likely to call themselves middle-class than their light-viewing (less than two hours daily) counterparts.

Overall, the Annenberg researchers found that television exerts a homogenizing effect.

Viewing blurs traditional differences, blends them into a more homogeneous mainstream, and bends the mainstream toward a "hard line" position on issues dealing with minorities and personal rights. Hard-nosed commercial populism, with its mix of restrictive conservatism and pork-chop liberalism, is the paradoxical—and potentially volatile—contribution of television to political orientations.[11]

This shaping of reality is not a matter of chance. Some years ago, at FCC hearings in 1965 to determine how much influence advertisers had on non-commercial content of television and radio, representatives of Proctor and Gamble testified to a set of quite explicit rules for television programs in which they would advertise.

There will be no material on any of our programs which could in any way further the concept of business as cold, ruthless, and lacking all sentiment or spiritual motivation.

If a businessman is cast in the role of villain, it must be made clear that he is not typical but is as much despised by his fellow businessmen as he is by other members of society.[12]

This is not extraordinary; if I were a major advertiser on television, I know how I would like psychiatrists to be portrayed.

However, obeying the Procter and Gamble guidelines required a distortion of reality, especially as P&G's instructions went beyond issues of the businessman's image. "Where it seems fitting, the characters in Procter and Gamble's dramas should reflect recognition and acceptance of the world situation in their thoughts and actions, although in dealing with war, our writers should minimize the 'horror' aspects."[13] These instructions further specified that "some basic conception of the American way of life" must not be attacked by a character in a drama or documentary unless a rejoinder is "completely and convincingly made someplace in the same broadcast." Finally, TV executives were instructed, "If there is any question whatever about such material, it should be deleted." P&G were protecting not just the business world, but also the general status quo.

That was twenty-five years ago, but the situation may not be different today as the media, especially newspapers, have become more and more dependent on advertiser revenues. Advertisers do not hesitate to threaten withdrawal of ads. In the case of major advertisers, such as the tobacco industry, the threat appears to be quite potent. Edith Whalen, a journalist with the American Council on Science and Health, reported in 1980 that she had approached the leading women's magazines (*Cosmopolitan, Harper's Bazaar, Ladies Home Journal, Mademoiselle, Ms., McCall's, Redbook, Seventeen, Vogue, and Working Woman*) asking them to run articles on the growing incidence of smoking-induced disease in women. All these magazines had run articles supporting the Equal Rights Amendment, but in this case they refused. Whelan commented, "I frequently wrote on health topics for women's magazines, and have been told repeatedly by editors to stay away from the subject of tobacco."[14]

As another example, Bagdikian reports that in 1981 a senior vice president of MGM told newspaper executives that there had been too many negative film reviews and that they could not take for granted the $500 million in ads that the industry place with them. Sounding much like Proctor and Gamble he warned, "Today the daily newspaper does not always create a climate that is supportive and favorable to the motion picture industry . . . gratuitous and hateful reviews threaten to cause the romance between newspapers and the motion picture industry to wither on the vine."[15]

More recently, the *San Francisco Chronicle* reported that the NBC television network cut off "Saturday Night Live" comedian Sam Kinison for about thirteen seconds, long enough to eliminate one joke. " 'They've taken the pot, there is no more pot,' Kinison said. 'You can't get any more pot. If you give us back the pot, we'll forget about the crack.' " The show's producer Lorne Michaels later explained, " 'They (the censors) didn't consider his drug references negative enough . . . The policy at NBC now is that the only references to drugs must be negative.' "[16]

Control of content is not exerted by advertising interests alone, but also by the owners of the media who hire and fire media personnel. Under normal circumstances media personnel have considerable latitude in what they present, but according to Bagdikian's research that latitude has its limits; what is not allowed is criticism of the free enterprise system itself. Writing in 1987, he commented:

> Some reporters often criticize specific corporate acts, to the rage of corporate leaders. But the taboo against criticism of the system of contemporary enterprise is, in its unspoken way, almost as complete within mainstream journalism and broadcast programming in the United States as criticism of communism is explicitly forbidden in the Soviet Union.[17]

He predicts that if the time came when corporations felt they were in fundamental jeopardy, nothing would prevent them from exercising their power of ownership to protect their interests.

Particularly in television, advertisers and the corporate world have been very influential in defining us to ourselves. The materialism and superficiality of most TV programs, and the emphasis on a world of middle-class whites between eighteen and forty-nine, is not necessarily what the public wants, as TV executives claim, but what the advertisers demand. Such covert indoctrination is typical of cults. In this instance it is not a particular religion or philosophy being served, but rather the enhancement of desire, the selling of products, the protection of the status quo. The effects of this indoctrination are a measure of the power of the media—and those who influence it—to shape our perception, to establish the climate of belief in which we live.

. ∎ ∎

Although they regard themselves as watchdogs in an adversarial role, media people are dependent on governmental authority because they rely heavily on access to the White House, Congress, and cabinet officials and on maintaining special relationships with contacts at the Pentagon, the Food and Drug Administration, or whatever government agencies are relevant to their assignments. The authorities can reward favored journalists with inside information and news scoops or penalize them by denying access. Bernard Roshco described a type of incident that occurs frequently enough to remind reporters that cooperation is essential to their livelihood. At a 1969 Nixon press conference, Stuart Loory, then the *Los Angeles Times'* White House correspondent questioned the president:

> In response to the President's statement that he favored neither instant segregation nor instant integration, Loory asked whether the years 1954 through 1968 could be termed "instant." The result was that Loory began losing his access to the news. He was dumped from the Air Force One press pool. On one Nixon trip to California, when the President invited several reporters to interview him while walking on the beach, Loory was left out even though his was the home paper and would have devoted much more space to the event. And *Los Angeles Times* reporters were not invited to Administration background briefings held to discuss the next year's State of the Union message.[18]

Consciously or unconsciously, every reporter must decide whether or not he or she wants to be another Stuart Loory. Without allowing themselves to notice, reporters may adjust their views or engage in internal censorship to minimize conflict with authority. Thus, their self-image of independence and objectivity can be preserved—and their access to the "source." Their suppression of dissent becomes unconscious.

All reporters assigned to a particular beat (for example, the Pentagon or the State Department) are subject to these influences. They need access to their sources, who in turn have their own needs for media attention. This mutual obligation system is likely to co-opt the reporter who, over time, becomes part of the institution he is covering. Warren Weaver, of the *New York Times,* pointed to this problem in his book *Both Your Houses.*

Institutional reporting has its advantages—members are more cooperative with reporters whom they come to sense as acolytes of the establishment—but the pitfalls are deep and dangerous. A reporter who has been admitted into the inner circle, or even allowed to peep in occasionally from the edge, is likely to be protective of the man who admitted him and of those observed there.[19]

A reporter may begin to identify with the source's point of view, to adopt a posture that is harmonious with the aims of the people he or she needs. News coverage is necessarily selective and the selection process may work unconsciously to omit items that would spoil a reporter's relationship with the source and to focus on those which will enhance it.

Mark Hertsgaard, a journalist who investigated the relationship between the press and the Reagan presidency, found a similar problem:

Indeed, the political effect of most news coverage was to fill people's heads with officially sanctioned truth. . . . This was to be expected; after all, the press took its definition of what constituted political news from the political governing class in Washington. Thus while the press *shaped* mass opinion, it *reflected* elite opinion; indeed, it effectively functioned as a mechanism by which the latter was transformed, albeit imperfectly, into the former.[20]

This unconscious process of accommodation and compliance is similar in kind to that which Hugh and Clara Robinson experienced in Life Force. Their dependence on Alex Monroe for advancement, favors, and continued status led them to support policies and behavior that they might otherwise have challenged. Their support of Alex was rationalized, using the group's dogma; critical thoughts were pushed aside.

■   ■   ■

On the one hand, media workers are interested in attracting the public interest by reporting dramatic conflicts in the social, economic, and political system of which they are a part. On the other hand, they are also interested in sustaining the system which produces the revenues that pay their salaries. The owners of the media feel comfortable with the establishment of which they are privileged members and in which they believe.

Media bias in favor of the status quo is often not obvious because of the appearance of debate in the various mass media presentations, especially network television. However, debate turns out to be within the rather narrow limits acceptable to authority. A recent study was conducted of the guest list of ABC's "Nightline." The analysis covered a forty-month period (1 January 1985 to 30 April 1988). Not counting ABC staff members, five guests appeared more than ten times: Henry Kissinger (fourteen), Alexander Haig (fourteen), Eliot Abrams (twelve), Jerry Falwell (twelve), Alejandro Bendana of Nicaragua's Foreign Office (eleven).

According to the study, this distribution is characteristic. Conservative and right-wing spokespersons, and government and ex-government officials dominated the airtime. Left-wing, "radical" spokespersons were usually from foreign countries. (Counting only American guests who appeared more than five times, there were nineteen, all men. The woman who appeared most frequently was Jean Kirkpatrick. All guests were white except for Jesse Jackson and Harry Edwards. Of the nineteen who appeared frequently, thirteen were conservative, most connected in some way to the Reagan administration. Labor, public interest, and social or ethnic leaders accounted for only 5.7 percent of the U.S. guest list.)[21]

Such bias can be quite invisible to the editors and producers themselves. Their pride and belief in their independence reflects the fact that they are rarely subject to crude arm twisting as to what or what not to present to the public. But their dependence on media owners and the government elite for financial rewards, information, and position can exert an insidious form of control— as it does in cults. The whole process can take place automatically, smoothly, even for those with more time for considered decisions then the average gatekeeper. Fred Freed, a producer of outstanding NBC public affairs programs reflected, "I have never been turned down for a program I wanted to do for censorship reasons. On the other hand I'm not sure I have ever asked to do one I knew management would not approve for these reasons."[22]

The result of media self-censorship is a tendency toward perpetuation of the assumptions fundamental to the government and business interests on which the media depend. This can have particularly farreaching consequences in foreign affairs. During the early years of the Vietnam War most within the media did not question cold war ideology, but continued to present the government's picture of a world divided into two camps, the free world and the communist, the latter assumed to be directed by Moscow through proxie armies in China, Cambodia, Vietnam, and elsewhere. This simplistic, ahistorical view supported the domino theory and justified intervention all over the world as vital to United States interests. Political scientist Daniel Hallin, who studied the role of the media during the Vietnam War, found that TV coverage did not often directly confront administration premises. Commentators and journalists disputed the effectiveness of government policies, but, all in all,

> none of the larger questions posed by the war was raised in any substantial way in the news. There was no discussion of the origins of revolution. . . . There was no second look at the doctrine of containment or its application to a conflict like Vietnam.[23]

Late in the war, when pressure for withdrawal began to mount, the media shifted to a more oppositional stance, but still within certain limits.

> Vietnam fits a pattern that has often been observed in situations of political crisis: the media in such periods typically distance themselves from incumbent officials and their policies, moving in the direction of an "adversary" conception of their role. *But they do not make the "system"—or its core beliefs—an issue, and if these are questioned, usually rise to their defense* [emphasis added].[24]

A similar situation prevailed in most coverage of the Iran hostage crisis during the Carter administration. Sociologist David Altheide found that "the Iranian situation was reduced to one story—the freeing of the hostages—rather than coverage of its background and context, of the complexities of Iran, of alternative American policies, and of contemporary parochial politics in a world dominated by superpowers."[25]

Daniel Hallin concludes that "this is one of the most important consequences of the close connection between the modern media and government: the range of political discussion in the press is usually restricted to the policy alternatives being debated in Washington."[26]

Economist Edward Herman and Noam Chomsky, philosopher and linguist, did extensive research on media coverage of Latin America and Indochina. They found a consistent pattern of "worthy and unworthy" victims. As an example, they contrasted the news coverage of the murder of a Polish priest, Jerszy Popieluszko, killed by the Polish police in October 1984, with the coverage of the murders of a large number of Latin American religious in El Salvador and Guatemala. The victims of communist governments received extensive coverage—they were apparently worthy. The victims of governments supported by the U.S. received scanty treatment, qualitatively different as well as much reduced in scope—they were apparently unworthy. The worthy received dramatic treatment and demands for justice; the unworthy mostly low-key, sparse descriptions accompanied by regrets about the violence from both left and right. The notion that the governments of Guatemala and El Salvador are reformist and centrist has been the official position of the Carter, Reagan, and Bush administrations, despite abundant evidence to the contrary. Herman and Chomsky make a compelling case for consistent media bias expressed with few exceptions through selective emphasis and by ignoring or downplaying contradictory testimony. The authors suggest that an additional factor may bias reporting on Latin America.

Western reporters are very rarely physically threatened—let alone murdered—in Poland, the Soviet Union, Cuba, or Nicaragua. They are often threatened and sometimes murdered in El Salvador, Guatemala, and other U.S. clients in Latin America. This irony is not commented upon in the free press, nor are the effects of this potential and actual violence against dissident reporters on the possibilities of honest reporting.[27]

Thus, there is much evidence that the mainstream mass media, controlled by corporate and financial interests, dominated by advertisers, and dependent on government sources generally reflects the point of view and interests of these groups. (There are notable exceptions, such as the CBS documentaries: *Hunger* and *The Selling of the Pentagon*, but covert conformity is the rule; in fact, these documentaries resulted in the network being investigated by the government agencies which they criticized.) As media commentator Herbert Gans observes, it is rare to read or see in the mainstream media any discussion of why wealth is distributed so unequally in our country and between the developing and developed nations, or of the power of corporations over the average citizen.[28]

How shall we understand the media's support of the status quo? Is the mass media just a propaganda machine, as Herman and Chomsky suggest? These authors show bias that exists, but they write as if media complicity is conscious. In some cases it may be, but I suggest that to a significant degree the processes that lead to bias operate outside awareness, as in cults; the politically correct and the economically expedient are internalized, become unconscious, and are reinforced by the group, which includes the public.

The assumptions that constitute the status quo are recycled for corporate owners, for advertisers, for government officials, as well as for the public. The limits defined by authorities are accepted unnoticed by almost everyone. Bagdikian concludes that "the butcher's thumb that quietly tilts news in favor of corporate values has survived the rise in journalistic standards. The tilt has been so quietly and steadily integrated into the normal process of weighing news that the angle of the needle is now seen as 'zero'."[29]

. . .

Within the corporate world, the more authoritarian the leadership structure, the less dissent is appreciated, and the more emphasis is given to loyalty to prevailing corporate views. Former General Motors executive John De Lorean describes how this loyalty was manifested:

> If your appearance, style and personality were consistent with the corporate stereotype, you were well on your way to being a "loyal" employee. But loyalty demanded more. It often demanded personal fealty, actual subservience to the boss . . .

Lower executives, eager to please the boss and rise up the corporate ladder, worked hard to learn what he wanted or how he thought on a particular subject. They then either fed the boss exactly what he wanted to know, or they modified their own proposals to suit his preferences.[30]

The devaluation and suppression of dissent can lead to financially disastrous corporate decisions or to violations of moral principles. The history of the Corvair is a case in point. As originally designed, the car had a tendency to flip over when making turns at high speed. According to John De Lorean, the problem was well known to the GM engineers, a number of whom fought to modify the car's suspension or keep it out of production. They were overruled by the general manager and finally told to stop objecting and "get on the team." The Corvair was produced and sold. De Lorean commented, "I don't think any one car before or since produced as gruesome a record on the highway as the Corvair."[31]

The costliest failure in the history of magazine publishing occurred when top executives of Time, Inc. pushed ahead with a project to publish a weekly broadcast and cable television listings magazine, *TV-Cable Week*, without the market testing recommended by their own researchers and without first solving major problems which other subordinates had brought to management's attention. A former member of the editorial management team described how adverse facts were shunted aside and deleted from the final presentation to the Board of Directors: "Sutton listened earnestly as Grum continued with his advice: keep the presentation simple, emphasize the up-side, and above all do not dwell on the complexities and uncertainties—the very risks that the task force had highlighted in the January presentation."[32]

Time, Inc. proceeded to lose $45 million on a magazine that ran for only six months. Not only did the board members uncritically accept the optimistic presentation, so did a Wall Street brokerage firm.

Munro and his associates were preaching to an audience that was eager to believe. One of the analysts at the gathering, Alan Gottesman, summed up his reaction to the presentation this way: "Hell, if you hear the company's top men say they've got some new breakthrough computer system to publish the magazine, you're going to believe them, right?"[33]

Wanting to believe is perhaps the most powerful dynamic initiating and sustaining cult-like behavior. Hugh and Clara Robinson accepted Alex Monroe's rationalizations for behavior that they would otherwise have labeled immoral, selfish, or cruel. Along with fear, the need to believe caused them to rationalize their own behavior and continue in Life Force long after the evidence of degeneration was in plain view to the outsider. A similar process seems responsible for the Corvair and *TV-Cable Week* fiascos. Dissenting voices that could have brought more reality to the decision-making process were ignored or suppressed. Wanting to believe affects everyone, leaders and followers alike.

The avoidance of dissent is almost automatic where unequal power exists and the leader makes it clear that being contradicted is displeasing, even dangerous. Dissent can only be utilized if the leader and the group value it, understand its necessity and demonstrate that dissent is welcome. In the corporate world, dissent is avoided and suppressed the more a CEO is unwilling to occupy an eye-level world with his subordinates and insists on their gazing upward at him.

The leader is not the only inhibiting force, the group as a whole can make its displeasure known if dissent focuses on areas of group vulnerability such as immoral corporate behavior, overoptimism, leadership mistakes, and paranoia. Even if a corporate CEO welcomes dissent, lower level executives may stifle contrary opinion so that it never reaches him or her. Something like this appears to have been responsible for the Challenger shuttle disaster. As described by Henry Cooper, Jr. in *The New Yorker*, Thiokol engineers voiced their concerns about the safety of the O-ring seal and believed the launch should be canceled, particularly as the air temperature at the launch site was lower than for any previous test measurements. Overruled by company officials, their objections were not passed on to those with final authority for the launch.[34]

Lower-level censorship is particularly likely when leadership wants condensed, simplified reports and summaries on which to base decisions. Unpleasant facts and possibilities are easier to prune and may be given shorter shrift than optimistic, forward-looking statements.

Avoidance of dissent is often confused with loyalty. Authoritarian leaders tend to regard loyalty as the foremost virtue of subordinates. Peter Wyden described how at the final meeting before the invasion of Cuba, Rusk, Nitze, and Bundy all set aside doubts and questions in order to "close ranks with the President" and vote in favor of the invasion.[35]

Only a lively appreciation of dissent's vital function at all levels of society can preserve it as a corrective to wishful thinking, self-inflation and unperceived rigidity.

■ ■ ■

In my view, the most prevalent current treatment of psychosis (in addition to reflecting devaluation of the outsider) demonstrates psychiatry's avoidance of dissenting views, its compliance with group pressures to maintain a particular belief system.

The current swing to a biological view of emotional illness has been described by Walter Reich, former research psychiatrist at the National Institutes of Mental Health, as "Psychiatry's Second Coming."[36] (The first was the oversell of the psychodynamic psychoanalytic approach.) The number of papers of a biological nature published in the *American Journal of Psychiatry* in 1980 was almost double that of ten years earlier. An even more noticeable shift has taken place in the *Archives of General Psychiatry*, which is now devoted almost exclusively to biochemical and genetic research. Furthermore, government support for drug research is heavily weighted toward research in genetics, biochemical causation of psychopathology, and drug therapy, while psychotherapeutic investigations receive relatively little funding.

Part of psychiatry's current ideology is that a person diagnosed as a schizophrenic is doomed to life-long social and work disability and recurrence of psychotic episodes unless treated with "anti-psychotic" drugs. This belief persists despite studies that indicate otherwise. Loren Mosher reviewed four long-term follow-up studies of patients treated *before the use of neuroleptic drugs* and found that they ". . . give us reason to be much more optimistic than we have been about outcome in schizophrenia. These 20-plus-year follow-up studies . . . yielded remarkably consistent results: 60%-85% of schizophrenic patients, depending on the criteria used, had achieved good social recovery."[37]

How could there be such good outcomes without the use of drugs? These studies challenge pessimistic beliefs concerning the prognosis of schizophrenia and call into question the necessity and desirability of drug treatment. The most prominent belief of the current biological psychiatry movement is that drugs are the treatment of choice for psychosis. This belief ignores the study by Bockhoven and Solomon comparing the five-year follow-up data of two groups of hospital patients, the first receiving psychological treatment (1947 to 1952, prior to the use of major tranquilizers) and the second group receiving drugs (1967 to 1972). No difference in outcome was found.

"This finding suggests that the attitudes of personnel toward patients, the socioenvironmental setting, and community helpfulness guided by citizen organizations may be more important in tipping the balance in favor of social recovery than are psychotropic drugs."[38]

These results were anticipated by Bockhoven's study of the results of "moral treatment," a humane, psychologically oriented hospital treatment program for the insane that flourished in the mid-nineteenth century.[39] Comparison of treatment results with present-day statistics suggests that moral treatment probably did as well or better than what is accomplished today with modern drug therapy.

Keeping these findings in mind it becomes apparent that psychiatry as a whole has avoided dealing with facts and opinions that challenge its ideology. Writing in the *Schizophrenia Bulletin*, John Kane cautions,

> Given the potential adverse effects that can be produced by antipsychotic drugs, it is critical that attention be given to the overall benefit to risk ratio when these agents are used. Although antipsychotic drugs may symptomatically improve a variety of conditions, they should not be used when equally effective and safer treatments are available.[40]

As the Bockhoven and Solomon research indicates, equally effective and safer treatments appear to be available for many patients. This is also suggested by other findings, some of which I have mentioned, but these data, discordant with the dominant ideology, fall on deaf ears.

When one considers the widespread reluctance of patients to take these drugs because of their distressing effects, the worsening of their condition that may take place, the disfigurement that may result and the equally good long-term outcome results of psychological treatment, the failure of psychiatry to take the dissenting data seriously is evidence of a cult-like ideology that shunts aside conflicting facts.

As in overt cults, psychiatry's embrace of an ideology limits realism. When a hospital patient becomes more agitated, noisy, combative and uncooperative the standard staff response is to increase the dosage of neuroleptic drug. Rarely is it considered that the patients' disturbance may reflect a conflict among the staff and that attention and corrective efforts should be directed there. Yet as early as 1956 Stanton and Schwartz had raised these issues in their landmark study of "institutional participation in psychiatric illness and treatment." They analyzed and documented many strong effects of hospital dynamics on the behavior of patients. "The most striking finding was that pathologically excited patients were quite regularly the subjects of secret, affectively important staff disagreement: and, equally regularly, their excitement terminated, usually abruptly, when the staff members were brought to discuss seriously their points of disagreement with each other."[41]

At the time the authors were hopeful and optimistic that their research would change the way inpatients were treated.

It has finally become clear that a mental hospital is a social system and that the meaning of any action taken within it can be known only if the context is known; it has become clear that many assumptions that had previously been taken for granted, such as the assumption that the mental hospital should take the general hospital as a model, are gratuitous and may be damaging. . . . Built solidly into procedures, techniques, and even the language of the mental hospital is the assumption that patients are mere passive objects of treatment; they are to be 'cared for,' 'protected,' 'treated,' 'respected,' 'handled,' 'controlled.' Psychiatric administrative language consistently speaks of the patient as if he were not actively participant, as if he were an unconscious or half-conscious body upon an operating table.[42]

When it comes to schizophrenia, what Stanton and Schwartz learned seems to have been forgotten; the awareness they hoped would change the mental hospital has not survived the Second Coming. Just as findings contradicting psychoanalytic assumptions were ignored by analytic theorists, so is work such as that of Stanton and Schwartz or Bockhoven and Solomon largely ignored today. Psychiatry as a profession does not censor discordant information but does ignore, dismiss, avoid it.

Of course, in pointing to those who apply only biological knowledge to the problem of psychosis and neglect the psychological, it should be recognized that there have been some psychiatrists who, drawing on R. D. Laing's ideas, have conceptualized acute schizophrenic psychosis as a "voyage of discovery," a means of spiritual development to be supported and not interfered with. Drugs are seen as only harmful and psychosis is romanticized. Maintaining such an ideology also requires one to ignore conflicting information, associating only with those who believe similarly and dismissing opponents as benighted.

■   ■   ■

The word *heretic* is derived from the Greek *hairetikos*, meaning "able to choose." All too frequently, administrators of religions consider themselves to be God's representatives and define any choice of doctrine or interpretation but theirs as false or evil. To the extent that religious leaders claim divine authority, dissent is discouraged and suppressed among their followers. Although differences of interpretation of holy writ always arise, when these differences are substantial they may not be tolerated. If dissenters are expelled or leave, a new religion may result; many different sects have arisen in all the major religions. When an individual defies doctrinal authority—becomes a heretic—and the difference in interpretation is deemed dangerous to the faith of true believers, punishment may be severe, barbaric. Muslim clergy tortured and killed Hallaj, the Sufi saint, for saying "I am God." Clergy of the Inquisition tortured and burned Christians who were far less challenging but were suspected of having the wrong beliefs.

Some choices are not permitted and dissent is punished, even in today's modern, pluralistic western world. A recent example is Pope John Paul II's attempt to banish dissent by revoking the right of a distinguished Catholic scholar, the Reverend Charles Curran, to teach at Catholic University. Curran had dissented at some points from non-infallible but traditional church teachings on sexual ethics. Archbishop Hickey explained the unusual and severe step taken by the Pope: ". . . the Holy See has gone on to clarify for us, to say there is no right to public dissent . . ."[43] A Vatican official commented further that "we now have a situation in the United States where many theologians teach not only church doctrine but also the dissident view . . . Then these professors ask the students to pick their choice . . . an absolutely unacceptable practice."[44]

Whatever one's position on dissent in the theological domain, it is clear that such an authoritarian attitude is incompatible with democratic government. Fundamentalist Jerry Falwell seems to agree, but finds the problem to be democracy itself.

> Today we find that America is more of a democracy than a republic. Sometimes there is mob rule. In some instances, a vocal minority prevails. Our Founding Fathers would not accept the tyranny of a democracy because they recognized that the only sovereign over men and nations was Almighty God.[45]

■　■　■

Members of almost all groups committed to a particular belief—be it religious or otherwise—are inclined to read and study works that confirm that belief. The dissenting views of outsiders are ignored or dismissed.

Where a religious group's security and the leader's power is heavily committed to infallibility, the extra precaution of direct censorship, including the burning of books, is taken, as occurred most recently in Iran. For centuries the Catholic Church maintained an Index of condemned books Catholics could not read without special permission because their faith or morals might be disturbed. Recently, Christian fundamentalists have tried to remove from American classrooms such diverse works as *Of Mice*

and Men, A Farewell to Arms, The Grapes of Wrath, 1984, Catch 22,
and even *The American Heritage Dictionary.*[46] There has been an on-
going battle to curtail the teaching of evolution and great concern
with the evils of "secular humanism."

To read or to listen to differing or opposing views is to court
disturbance, trouble, doubt. Billy Graham puts it thus: "The world
longs for authority, finality, and conclusiveness. It is weary of
theological floundering and uncertainty. Belief exhilarates the human spirit; doubt depresses."[47]

The exclusion of doubt has a price. Intellectual parochialism
may be fostered by restricting contact with outsiders and by building walls of indifference or, in the most extreme cases, hate.

When religions provide schooling for members' children, such
schools may isolate the children from other worldviews and facilitate a portrayal of the outsider as evil or inferior. When this educational insulation is perpetuated into adulthood, cult-like abuses
may arise. Until recently, the Catholic parochial school system
provided recruits for seminaries and convents which, in turn, provide teachers to perpetuate the school system. Although not all
parochial schools are repressive, many have created an atmosphere of fear, guilt, and conformity. As one former nun put it,
"You are taught that what is bad in you is yours; what is good in
you is God's."[48] The deadening effect of such an education is at-
tested to by ex-nuns' autobiographical accounts.

> I have been becoming more and more aware of the deadness I
> see all around me—the deadness of tired, tense bodies cling-
> ing to a ritual, of people who patch up life's cracks so nothing
> new can sink in. I see their intensity and I see their serious-
> ness; I see their compulsive concern for the slightest deviation
> from the Holy Rule. And what is most frightening, I see the
> hugeness and monstrosity of their commitment to suffering.[49]

Christianity is not alone in providing systems which shield
members from outside views. The Lubavitcher Hasidic community in Brooklyn is a case in point. Veneration of its leader ap-
proaches worship. The exclusiveness and separation of members
from the larger community, enforced by unusual dress, elaborate
rules and rituals, and specialized studies and language, can result
in an extremely narrow and parochial outlook which is, in essence, cult-like. In a long, mostly favorable article on the Hasidic

community, Liz Harris writes of being surprised when her host declared that he did not believe Jacobo Timerman's description of his incarceration and torture by Argentina authorities. Indeed, he declared there was no anti-Semitism in Argentina. The reason for his view was that Timerman was believed to be "sympathetic to the Communists". Since the communists were a godless people who persecuted Jews and Argentina at the time of the interview was certainly anti-communist, Timerman was not to be believed. Harris comments,

> I found it astonishing that one obvious reality, the suffering of Russian Jews, could utterly annihilate another, the suffering of Jacobo Timerman and many like him. Did it matter to Moshe that Timerman had emphatically denied any Communist sympathies? Or that fuzzy political accusations had brought about the disappearance of thousands of innocent people? The bright light that the Hasidim trained on their communal and inner life seemed to dim considerably when it was turned on the outside world—a circumstance that appeared to strain the quality of mercy hereabouts.[50]

Of course, the more a religion allows debate, discussion and disagreement, the more adaptable and realistic it can be, the less captured by its form. However, this tolerance may threaten certainty, and certainty (as Billy Graham testified) is one of the great attractions of religious belief.

■   ■   ■

Irving Janis, a psychologist who studied presidential advisory groups, notes that in Washington, as elsewhere, the suppression of deviant points of view is often done by subordinates to protect the President from discordant opinions that might damage their confidence. The underlying wish is to preserve for all the fantasy of the Leader.

Unless a leader clearly intends that subordinates should challenge and criticize, his or her views will meet little serious opposition. Hugh and Clara Robinson's story shows how cult followers, even without specific instructions, act to protect the position and views of their leader. In the capacity of protectors, group members may feel justified in employing threats, subterfuge, and deceit.

In our government, as in most, a principal means of avoiding dissent and criticism is through the use of secrecy. Nowhere has this been more manifest than in the planning of covert operations such as the the overthrow of Chilean President Salvadore Allende during the Nixon administration and the more recent disaster, the sale of arms to Iran during the Reagan administration.

Secrecy supports cult-like behavior, as we saw in the Life Force group, where the hierarchy was maintained through limiting access to information. Secrecy functions not only to cover up unethical activities from outside eyes, but also to increase authoritarian control over the larger group. By promoting the idea that the leader or the in-group have special information and expertise, they remove themselves from criticism and justify the exclusion of others from the decision-making process.

In the case of religious cults the special information and expertise is described as divine inspiration or enlightenment. The cult leader's presumed higher state precludes lower beings from judging his or her actions.[51] Similar claims are made in government where special knowledge of the enemy or secret technical information is said to justify decisions that would otherwise be objected to on moral or even practical grounds.

Secrecy is invoked often in the name of national security. Tom Wicker, *New York Times* columnist, comments on the connotations of that term, meanings we can understand in terms of cult psychology:

But those two words [national security] are magic, an incantation, vibrating with the ideas of power, knowledge, authority, responsibility. National security!—the phrase rings with masculinity, patriotism, heroism. Used in tones of proper solemnity by someone from the White House or the Pentagon, those words can mesmerize most Americans; and a generation of Washington reporters stood mostly in awe of them—not least, I believe, because a reporter who knows something that can't be printed for national-security reasons is elevated himself into that prized masculine circle of power, knowledge, authority, responsibility. He becomes the ultimate insider; and the reporter's deadliest enemy—the desire to be an accepted

part of the world of power around him—has won its final victory.[52]

.   .   .

As Americans, we affirm the right to dissent, consider it of supreme value, make the infringement of dissent unlawful, and recognize it as basic to our political system. However, in actual practice few of us are pleased when someone disagrees with us; at best
we tolerate it, inwardly we reject it. Although in our society the
right to dissent is constantly affirmed, there is little indication that
as individuals or in groups we value opposing views directed at
ourselves. In science, within clear professional limits, there may
be more appreciation of dissent, more readiness to welcome the
opponent, but in general, although we may defend the right of an
opponent to speak out against us we are not grateful when he or
she has done so. In almost all cases we react to dissent as to an
enemy, countering with argument or a patronizing dismissal. This
seems natural, just "human nature." Yet, considering how much
of our thinking is prejudiced, rigid, and self-protective and how
much we make use of inadequate and selective information, dissent deserves to be treated not as an adversary but as an ally,
something that can rescue us from selective blindness, make us
more realistic and thus more effective. Objectively, we should regard dissent with gratitude. It is a matter of some chagrin to me
that even in the process of writing this book I find it very difficult
to practice what I preach; whenever my own opinions are challenged my first response is to put up my mental fists and fight
back, defending my position. Only then do I catch myself and ask
the dissenter, Why do you think that?

Look around at all levels of society. The adversarial approach
is ingrained; authors, radio and television commentators, spokespersons for various causes, politicians of every hue, all insist on
the rightness of their own views while denigrating the opposition's. Yet life is complex; our perception and information are limited. Indeed, to some degree, everyone is in error.

Just like the members of Life Force, we want agreement for
our beliefs so we can feel the security of being right. Dissent
threatens that, it reduces our status, our certainty, our claim to

privilege. As I remarked earlier, the problem with Reagan's "evil empire" speech was not so much that he was harshly critical of the Soviet government—surely it deserved harsh criticism—but that he did not acknowledge that we as a nation are not free from evil, even if our system is more humane.

In all the deservedly adverse comment that Reagan received for that speech, there was no recognition that similar speeches take place every day in the utterances and opinions of almost all citizens, liberal and conservative alike. Many people regarded Reagan and his conservative allies as the source of evil in this country, oblivious to the irony that in doing so they were engaging in similar thinking. Again, the key issue is not that criticism is undeserved, but that the persons dishing out criticism reserve none for themselves, nor do they acknowledge any validity to the other's position. They are not being artful. They simply cannot accept the fact that their adversary has the same self-righteous feeling as they do because the implications are uncomfortable: our own feelings of sincerity and righteousness do not certify that we are right. To welcome dissent is to accept that fact.

In ordinary life, dissent is restricted primarily by a selective focus on the familiar and the comfortable. At the same time, there may be more restriction by exclusion than we realize. In 1946, when I was in high school, a Russian Communist was invited to address our weekly assembly. I remember that we were unconvinced by his protestations that the USSR wanted only peace. Afterwards students joked, "Yeah, a piece of Poland, a piece of Hungary and a piece of Germany." We were surprised to hear that the American Legion was upset that he had been allowed to speak to us. What are they afraid of? we thought. He hadn't captured our minds.

Some years later, after the Korean War, I heard a talk by a former American soldier who had been a POW and had gone over to the Chinese Communists. They had treated him well, given him a job and even a daily glass of milk, which they understood to be necessary for Americans. But he found the conformity oppressive, became very homesick and returned to the United States. He said he had been susceptible to their arguments because, coming from a small Midwestern town, he had never heard the United States criticized and was impressed that some of their criticism was undeniably true.

Hearing this man, I realized he rebutted the American Legion's concern. Not having been exposed to dissident views, he had been a sitting duck for skillful propaganda; indeed, most of those who were similarly won over were from unsophisticated environments. I thought then how much we needed dissent.

Yet I doubt that many American high schools during the last three decades have invited a Communist to address their assembly. Since the McCarthy period we seem less tolerant of challenges to our basic political principles. The Socialist Party is all but non-existent in America; political statements are tame and court the national consensus; free enterprise is not challenged. We pride ourselves on freedom of dissent but there is not much serious dissent in our politics, nor in the national media. Radical voices tend to be dismissed as lunatic. It's a free country, but we are as free to turn our backs on dissent as to express it.

In ordinary society, the cult processes of censorship and decreased contact with outsiders are often found, but in diminished intensity. Censorship of discordant information and isolation from heretical outsiders is usually done voluntarily rather than at the insistence of the group, although the expression of deviant views is seldom encouraged. Bankers tend to associate with bankers, doctors with doctors, sergeants with sergeants, black with black, and so on. Similarly for various socio-economic, ethnic, and religious groups. These associations provide not only shared interests, but also the security of support for one's views. Furthermore, liberals and conservatives tend to confine their reading to those magazines and columnists whose views are similar to their own; if they scan the writings of the opposition it will be to attack and disparage, not to learn. At their political gatherings one seldom hears a serious questioning of the group's beliefs or any acknowledgement that opponents may be correct in a particular instance. Instead, what takes place is an exercise in mutual support and validation, a reinforcing of the group's belief in the correctness of its views, a strengthening of the fantasy of being true, good and superior. A de facto censorship operates continuously. Whatever the cause of these social ghettos, their effect is to deny a person the benefit of being challenged and contradicted.

Exit from the Cult

CULT behavior is present throughout society but is particularly evident in the military, whose fanatical support of the arms race has led us to the brink of extinction. The wish of military leaders for power and their training in destruction cause them to imagine enemies where there are none and to exaggerate the aggressive intentions of others. The military cult attempts to glorify war and is ready to sacrifice millions of lives for the abstraction of victory. Thus, generals and admirals are enthusiasts of nuclear weapons and think of them not much differently than the toy guns they fired gleefully as children—the bigger the better. For this reason, we must be aware of the influence and manipulation employed by the military establishment in order to maintain power and promote war. If we can see what is happening to us, we can take action to prevent them from leading us to nuclear disaster.

We are all susceptible to cult processes. Did you agree with what I said above about the military? I was purposefully devaluing them, using the same means that cults employ to define an outside group as evil. The attributions I made were exaggerated generalizations. Do you know any high-ranking military officers? It is possible that the paragraph above fits them, but most likely it does not.

Consider the phrase "the military, whose fanatic support of the arms race has led us to the brink of extinction." It permits no distinctions among members of the military, no recognition that opinions and motives vary from person to person, as in any other group. Such stereotyping cannot account for statements such as this one on nuclear weapons:

> At the theatre or tactical level any nuclear exchange, however limited it might be, is bound to leave NATO worse off in comparison to the Warsaw Pact, in terms both of military and civilian casualties and destruction . . . To initiate use of nuclear weapons . . . seems to me to be criminally irresponsible.[1]

The person quoted is Field Marshall Lord Carver, Chief of the British Defense Staff from 1973 to 1976. He is not the only powerful military officer to take that position. Admiral Hyman Rickover, the principal force behind the development of the nuclear submarine fleet, on the occasion of his retirement, advocated doing away with nuclear weapons and nuclear reactors as well.

> The most important thing we could do is start by having an international meeting where we first outlaw nuclear weapons, and then we outlaw nuclear reactors, too . . . I think it would be the finest thing in the world for the President of the United States to immediately initiate another disarmament conference . . . this is a very propitious time, when the military expenses are eating up so much of the people's taxes.[2]

Nor is Rickover an exception among the American military. Gene LaRocque, another retired admiral, is a leading speaker for Physicians for Social Responsibility and heads the Center for Defense Information, a peace movement organization. And what are we to make of the fact that in May 1982 the entire Joint Chiefs of Staff supported reductions in strategic nuclear arsenals in opposition to Secretary of Defense Caspar Weinberger, a civilian? Around the same time, the chairman of the Joint Chiefs supported the peace movement in its pressure for arms control. "Opponents of nuclear weapons in the United States 'are not a fringe element' but contain many who support a strong military and still want 'to get on with some arms control that is meaningful and results in very substantial reductions.' "[3] The military acted as a moderating force when the Joint Chiefs of Staff opposed President Reagan's wish to send a battleship group to South America.

My use of the term "fanatical" denigrates and devalues the opposing view by attacking the character of the opponent rather than addressing the content of what is proposed. A fanatic is "a person possessed by an excessive and irrational zeal, especially for a religious or political cause."[4] With the use of this term, advocacy of an arms buildup becomes "irrational zeal," without the writer having to prove that it is so. My demonstration paragraph contains no attempt to understand what legitimate basis might exist for the military's advocacy of an increased arms budget; that viewpoint is only condemned or devalued. The fact is, a general or an admiral might believe that a nuclear war would be an utter disaster for his country, but that an increased arms budget would help guard against such a war. And it is at least possible that such thinking might be correct. Some generals argue strongly for building up conventional forces rather than nuclear arms.

The sample paragraph given above does not acknowledge or discriminate among these possibilities. Instead, it attempts to establish a separate class of human beings, "the military", characterized as wrong or bad—people not like us. The reader is always included in the "us" because in cult communication us means good. We usually do not challenge such an inclusion even though its purpose is to exclude someone else, to lead us to regard them as bad or, at the least, inferior. This is a typical illustration of devaluation as it occurs in everyday life.

The second sentence of the paragraph establishes that the military has bad motives, "The wish of military leaders for power and their training in destruction causes them to imagine enemies where there are none and to exaggerate the aggressive intentions of others." Thus they want power and destruction and are paranoid to boot. The problem with this statement is projection. The sentence implies that the bad traits it designates characterize the military rather than anyone else, not the writer, and by unspoken agreement, not the reader. That implication is certainly false. A keen interest in violence and destruction can be found in almost everyone—witness the continued popularity of shoot-em-up, beat-em-up television and movie entertainment. In what seems to be the favorite plot, the villain has been so bad that the hero has license to behave brutally, cruelly and vindictively, violating all precepts of fairness or legality in the process. Judging by the Neilson ratings, military personnel do not comprise the total audience for such blood-fests.

The capacity for violence, physical or psychological, is present in all human beings. At the same time, everyone thinks of themselves as having good intentions. Indeed, after many years as a psychiatrist, it is clear to me that most human beings, *especially* those whose behavior is abhorrent, are likely to think of themselves as victims rather than villains, misunderstood by others, not appreciated, treated unfairly, not deserving the hardships encountered. It is doubtful that anyone rises in the morning exclaiming, "Aha! Another day to be evil!"

The wish for personal power is also universal and not confined to the military. As a liberal I have attended many peace movement meetings and have observed that being on a platform brings out the demagogue in many speakers and leaders, whether of the right, left, or center. I myself enjoy giving lectures to large groups of people and still remember one gathering of a thousand that responded with such enthusiasm that I could understand how Benito Mussolini must have felt when he spoke from his balcony. Power, vanity, and greed can flower exuberantly even while high-minded words are being declaimed. (I haven't attended any conservative or right-wing rallies but have observed them on television and read the speeches delivered there. The effect of the platform on the speaker is the same.)

The second sentence of our sample attributes a paranoid perspective to the generals and admirals ("to imagine enemies where there are none"). Quite possibly this does occur in the military, depending on the person and the circumstances, but this too is true of everyone else. Indeed, paranoia depends on attributing to some one or some group precisely those traits one denies in oneself and the reader who accepted the opening paragraph did just that. The paragraph offers a good example of unnoticed, everyday projection, a basic cult dynamic. In this example the generals and admirals are the focus of projection, but just as often the peace movement, the "doves", "the left" are designated as bad, inferior, irresponsible.

An interesting exercise is to consult the newspaper columnists, magazines, or television commentators that are your preferred sources of information and notice the devaluation and projection that is employed—with your tacit approval—when Washington politics, the Soviet Union, nuclear war, or other controversial subjects are discussed. The devaluation reinforces your sense of rightness and establishes a clear source of evil. Also observe the tone of righteousness that accompanies such cult behavior. It signals the presence of projection; They are bad (we are good). You may notice in yourself the fantasy that if you were in power things would be done right!

The last two sentences of the chapter's opening paragraph sound a warning that is true enough ("we must be aware of the devices of influence and manipulation employed"), but that applies to everyone—the military, the peace movement, the Left and the Right, blacks and whites, Christians, Jews, and Muslims, rich and poor.

The military is authoritarian by nature and will inevitably manifest some of the cult behavior we have seen in religions, large corporations, and other social institutions. What is most important is that each of us become more aware of his or her own cult thinking. Only through such awareness can we extricate ourselves from the invisible, everyday cults of which we are members.

.   ∎   ∎

The opening paragraph of this chapter was written to provide an experience of cult thinking by appealing to and stimulating the reader's likely prejudices, fears, and wishes. I used such a device because personal bias tends to make influence and manipulation invisible to those affected. If you are a member of the military or a hard-line conservative, you may not have been swayed; however, for many of us, characterizing generals and admirals as warmongering, stupid, or callous fits our projections very nicely. We consider ourselves, in contrast, to be peace-loving, intelligent, and empathic. We cannot grant laudable characteristics to people advocating very different views without raising the possibility that they could be correct and we in error.

Your response may be, That's nothing new; I know all that. Indeed, the concept of cult behavior can be easily grasped, but *experiencing* it in one's own thinking and behavior is a different matter. Intellectuals in particular, who are trained not to be caught off balance by any idea, may find the concepts of cult psychology overly familiar and yet continue with their own cult behavior and be as ignorant of it as the members of Life Force. If you still feel immune from cult influence, I can offer a checklist of everyday behaviors that you may recognize all too well:

1. Speaking of adversaries or outsiders (e.g., conservatives, liberals, Yuppies, blue-collar, rich, poor) as if they were all the same; characterizing them by negative traits only; attributing unflattering motives to them but not to oneself.

2. Lacking interest and information concerning the actual statements and actions of opponents or outsiders.

3. Failing to consider the possible validity of an adversary's point of view.

4. Not taking a critical look at one's own position.

5. Disapproving or rejecting a member of one's group for departing from the group position, devaluing the dissident, regarding him or her as an annoyance or a problem.

6. Feeling self-righteous.

■   ■   ■

Exit from the invisible cult is very important because cult thinking has such serious consequences, especially at the government level. In her book, *March of Folly*, Barbara Tuchman presents striking examples of both ancient and modern governments that persisted in disastrous policies while ignoring correct advice and countervailing experience. She blames this primarily on "woodenheadedness."

> Wooden-headedness, the source of self-deception, is a factor that plays a remarkably large role in government. It consists in assessing a situation in terms of pre-conceived fixed notions while ignoring or rejecting any contrary signs. It is acting according to wish while not allowing oneself to be deflected by the facts.[5]

We can recognize here a description of one of the basic cult behaviors, avoiding dissenting views. Correspondingly, in Tuchman's list of requirements for reasonable leadership we see the opposite—a readiness to learn, to acknowledge error,

> to keep well-informed, to heed information . . . if the mind is open enough to perceive that a given policy is harming rather than serving self-interest, and self-confident enough to acknowledge it, and wise enough to reverse it.[6]

The only hope Tuchman sees for averting further government folly is that the electorate be educated to select leaders by recognizing and rewarding integrity of character—moral courage—and rejecting "the ersatz." She is not sanguine about this possibility and concludes, somewhat helplessly, "We can only muddle on."

Actually, we are not that helpless. The study of cult psychology and its manifestations in ordinary life provides a framework with which to understand *why* wooden-headedness exists, *what* the behavior of a competent leader is, and *how* we can educate both leaders and electorate to do more than muddle on. The necessary information is available. If we allow ourselves the awareness of our wish for shepherds, our longing for the back seat of the car, then we have a much better chance of avoiding folly.

. . .

Beyond heightening such awareness, there are some specific ways to reduce cult behavior in society. One of the most effective would be to promote anti-authoritarian education. As I have argued, our initial social experience in the family sets the pattern for the roles of leader and follower and we readily create a parent out of anyone who seeks to lead, teach, or command. We elevate such a person, just as we looked up to our parents who were literally above us. Authoritarian leaders stimulate and intensify this response.

A young child's critical evaluation of his or her parent is very difficult because the child's understanding is limited by an egocentric view that relates all events to himself or herself as cause. A child cannot comprehend the network of forces affecting parents and their society; furthermore, critical evaluation may be hazardous and frightening. When a child accurately perceives hypocrisy, selfishness, or irrationality in the parent—and says so—he or she risks punishment and the parent's withdrawal. Even the awareness of a parent's bad actions may be intolerable, for the parent is the young child's world and if the world is bad, what hope can be maintained? For this reason, children often regard themselves as bad rather than see the failings of a mother or father; in adulthood, when faced with the harmful behavior of an idealized leader, reality may again be denied.

The fact is, the capacity for objective assessment of leaders and authorities is not developed in many homes or schools. Although historical figures or current political leaders may be discussed, the role and power of parents and teachers seldom is. Authorities of any kind rarely encourage an objective appraisal of themselves. In consequence, as adults we may be vulnerable to the unrealistic claims of charismatic, authoritarian leaders. But this can be changed, if we wish, and the place to begin is in the schools.

For educational institutions to give up authoritarian power and abandon indoctrination may seem impossible, but the research of Gerda Lederer and others on post–World War II German youth provides evidence that such a goal is achievable. After World War II, authoritarianism (defined by Lederer as a readiness to submit to authority combined with a readiness to dominate those with less power) was recognized as an important factor in the rise of the Nazis and the willingness of German citizens to follow wherever Hitler led. Beginning in the 1960s, a deliberate effort was made in West Germany to reduce or eliminate the authoritarian attitude.

> Most of the Nazi-era schoolteachers were dismissed because of party membership. Most of the old textbooks were destroyed. Beyond that, educational leaders set out to do what had not been done after World War I, during the Weimar Republic: totally change the atmosphere of the schools so as to practice democratic values as well as preach them.[7]

When Lederer arrived in West Germany to do her research (originally on the difference in math scores between American and

German students), she was required to take a month-long teacher training course.

The training emphasized that the students, not the teachers, should do most of the talking in the classroom. "We do not use the frontal approach in teaching," the German instructor said. "Don't expect your students to be quiet and listen." The students should be encouraged to talk among themselves, he added.[8]

The atmosphere was so different from the stereotype of German discipline that Lederer felt like Alice in Wonderland. In 1978, using a carefully constructed questionnaire, she found that, in contrast to the findings in 1945, West German adolescents were on a par with American adolescents with regard to authoritarianism. Both groups had shown a significant reduction in authoritarian beliefs between 1945 and 1978, but the West Germans' change had been more dramatic; where there were differences in 1978, the West German adolescents showed a greater support for democratic values than did the American students! (The poll research confirmed the similar findings of a massive, multinational study conducted in 1971 by the International Association for the Evaluation of Educational Achievement [IEA].)

This apparently successful effort on the part of West German authorities to teach anti-authoritarianism suggests that schools can encourage students to examine the roots of their automatic obedience to authority (and of automatic rebellion as well). Considered most broadly, this could be seen as an education in anti-cult psychology. However, it must be recognized that teaching students to perceive and understand the operations of authoritarianism requires more than the establishment of a democratic classroom. I believe that the process of observation and reflection should be applied to the reactions of students and teachers to the social structures of their own educational milieu, of their peer groups, of their families. They would need to learn about the indoctrination and bias present in their society which is communicated directly via news and opinion sources and indirectly via entertainment and advertising. Then they would be in a position to study cults per se, and relate them to themselves. They would begin to understand the forces shaping their beliefs and values. In the words of Idries Shah, "People are widely held to have the right to attack what they dislike. We have not yet, however, reached the stage where it is required that people understand (though they purport to describe) the roots of liking and disliking."[9]

· · ·

Allied to anti-authoritarian education is the fostering of autonomy in various sectors of society, which can also help limit the extent of cult behavior by encouraging the expression in action of multiple individual viewpoints. Autonomy is a mark of adulthood, whereas subservience and automatic deference are marks of childlike dependency. As we have seen, cults regress their members to a stage of dependency on the group and child-like expectations of the leader, who is elevated far above the followers and regarded as if he or she were infinitely wise.

The issue of autonomy is important in the corporate world. The most successful companies appear to have achieved a balance between autonomy and centralized control such that neither dimension gets out of hand. Alfred Sloan at General Motors had such a goal.

> A delicate balance was to be maintained between the freedom of the various operations to manage their business, competing internally as well as outside the company, and the controls necessary to coordinate these operations in the best interests of the corporation's growth and performance.[10]

The Japanese have been very successful at achieving a similar balance. An executive of one of Japan's largest suppliers of electrical products describes their approach:

> Matsushita fosters autonomy and provides enormous incentive for group and individual performance. But . . . Matsushita exercises extraordinarily tight control over a few variables. The planning process, and in particular the six-month operating plan, are taken very seriously.[11]

> Matsushita believes that people can be trusted. However, our control system provides guidelines to prevent ruinous mistakes.[12]

Another company, Schlumberger, provides us with clear examples of how autonomy is given employees and how much they value it. In the words of several of their field engineers,

The thing that drew me here was that no other job gives you the responsibility you are given here right out of school.

I have much more responsibility than I would in other jobs. The technical side is quite interesting. The engineer has his own unit, his own tools, his own team.

I joined because I wanted to go overseas and have my own show.

I have the impression that I'm running my own company.[13]

The excellent companies studied by Peters and Waterman all worked to treat their employees with respect, to regard them as adults rather than unruly, lazy children. Initiative, autonomous decision making, and constructive disagreement were encouraged. Sloan's genius at General Motors was to organize independent divisions in control of their own operations but responsive to headquarters' long-range planning. (After Sloan, more and more decision making was taken over by a headquarters staff that had less and less experience in the manufacture and sale of automobiles. Multiple committees intervened to delay decisions and thereby lose both opportunities and money.)[14]

▪ ▪ ▪

The informed voter is supposed to be the bedrock of democracy, but an interesting study of citizen voting habits done in the 1950s suggests that the rational, objectively interested citizen does not really exist.[15] The researchers concluded that it is the ill-informed, relatively indifferent voters who are essential for a liberal democracy, that only they are responsive to changing conditions, providing flexibility to the body politic. The well-informed, highly interested, involved citizen is usually quite partisan and unmoved by argument; on the left and the right, such stalwarts anchor the political ship, providing stability.

Highly interested voters vote more, and know more about the campaign, and read and listen more, and participate more; however, they are also less open to persuasion and less likely to change. Extreme interest goes with extreme partisanship and might culminate in rigid fanaticism that could destroy democratic processes if generalized throughout the community.[16]

This somewhat disconcerting finding is due in part to the fact that what informs the citizen is largely propaganda issuing from one side or the other. Radio, television, magazines, and newspapers feature both critics and defenders of a particular policy, but each of these selects facts useful to his or her position, emphasizes certain principles and ignores others, often evoking emotional responses, prejudices, and fears. After reading or hearing such a presentation one may be persuaded, influenced, or won over, but one is not really better informed if what one has encountered is not essential information, but convincing propaganda.

Unless the audience knows a great deal about the subject, one-sided presentations can be very persuasive. In most conflict situations, disagreements are based on differences in interpretation and in the priorities given to different values; but these differences are seldom stated, and, lacking that clarification, we absorb highly selective information, are swayed to one side or the other, but end up no wiser.

As Jacques Ellul points out, whether propaganda is democratic or totalitarian does not matter, choice and discrimination are damaged.

> The existence of two contradictory propagandas is no solution at all . . . the individual is not independent in the presence of two combatants between whom he must choose. He is not a spectator comparing two posters, or a supreme arbiter when he decides in favor of the more honest and convincing one . . . The individual is seized, manipulated, attacked from every side; the combatants of two propaganda systems do not fight each other, but try to capture *him*.[17]

Opposing propagandas do not assist the democratic process but produce partisans, each with the mind-set of a cult member who

> demands simple solutions, catchwords, certainties, continuity, commitment, a clear and simple division of the world into Good and Evil, efficiency, and unit of thought. He cannot bear ambiguity. He cannot bear that the opponent should in any way whatever represent what is right or good. . . . the

individual will escape either into passivity or into total and unthinking support of one of the two sides.[18]

In order for the citizen to exercise a realistic choice a more searching alternative is needed, *a making use of dissent* as a way of raising the level of informed judgment without raising the level of partisanship. Let us imagine a debate or discussion the goal of which is to clarify a controversial problem and proposed solutions. The focus would be on the fundamental questions of how the data are interpreted and what values are given priority. The intent would not be to overwhelm or capture the audience, but to clarify the competing values that are involved in the conflict and in the proposed solutions. In this way we could become informed without becoming opinionated. Logically, four areas would be clarified:

1. The key data (Are they disputed?)
2. Interpretations of the data.
3. Value conflicts. (Reason for giving one value priority over the other?)
4. Error indicators. (What events or facts would indicate to each side that their belief or strategy should be changed?)

. . .

The best corporate executives promote real dissent even though they may find it irritating. Harold Geneen, who ruled ITT like an absolute monarch, was nevertheless quite clear about the importance of dissent and said that he deliberately fostered it in his search for "the unshakeable facts."

> We cut through layers of fat in our management ranks by putting all the people in one room so they could talk with one another, face to face, regardless of rank, and an honest assessment of any situation could be based upon the facts which emerged.
>
> But that is only the surface of the matter. Beneath that surface was the clear understanding that we *owed* each other our honest opinions at all times. People could disagree with me or with anyone else; they could criticize me or anyone else, and

no one would suffer as a consequence. I tried to welcome criticism. Naturally, no one *likes* to be criticized. One's first instinct is to be defensive and fight back. But that is the kind of defensiveness one should try to keep under control. I consciously tried to lean over backwards to avoid bridling when someone disagreed with me. I always wanted someone to point out where I might be heading for a mistake. I never batted down such a man. I listened and we exchanged views . . . But more important than the encounter itself was that at meetings others observed what was happening and word got around the company that one could speak his mind, disagree with the boss, and be heard.[19]

Geneen's description of himself receives support from ITT executives whom Pascale and Athos interviewed.

"Geneen didn't mistrust people in a misanthropic sense," says one senior-level manager. "But he did mistrust a single source." Geneen disliked relying on one perspective as the means for giving him the whole picture. He believed that people have different points of view and that it is dangerous to listen to a small coterie.[20]

[Referring to the face-to-face confrontations that were encouraged at large executive meetings:] It was like a tennis match; you could play an aggressive game with your opponent but still have a relationship with him when their game was over.[21]

Jean Riboud, when CEO of Schlumberger, picked key people who were not afraid to disagree with him, people who had "the courage of their convictions," who did not "float like a cork," but "force[d] people to think." Ed Carlson, who was CEO of United Airlines, also valued dissent.

When Carlson was in accord with his advisors, he might play devil's advocate to see if he could support the opposite side with logic. "He sought the difference of opinion among his executives," said one observer, "and anyone in the group was expected to disagree loudly if he felt so disposed." Carlson's only rule: Disagree without being disagreeable.[22]

Contrast these attitudes with those of the General Motors executives described by De Lorean, or the imperial manner of Henry

Ford II as described by Lee Iacocca in his autobiography,[23] or the behavior of key executives during the *TV-Cable News* fiasco.[24] Inhibiting dissent can be as costly in industry as it is in cults.

■ ■ ■

Fostering dissent and recognizing its value are essential to realistic decision making. It is true that authoritarian decision-makers who dispense with dissent can be right in their decisions; but they can also be very wrong. General Douglas MacArthur showed brilliant independent judgment during the Korean War in his insistence on an amphibious assault of Inchon despite the unanimous objections of the Joint Chiefs of Staff. In that case he was right. However, according to historian William Manchester, MacArthur's equally strong belief during World War II that he would defeat the Japanese on the Lingayen beaches northwest of Manila led him to delay shifting vast stores of food and supplies to Bataan (as originally planned by the Joint Chiefs for a retreat and holding action). Finally, when it was too late to supply the peninsula, MacArthur retreated; but the troops, who otherwise would have been able to hold out for years, were starved into surrender and most died on the Death March.[25]

Today, nuclear weapons have made the stakes of government decision making higher than in the past. Only responsible dissent, voiced and listened to, can offer protection against cataclysmic error. With this need in mind, Irving Janis has suggested adopting procedures aimed at facilitating dissent in government. Among the steps he recommends are:

> Assign the role of critical evaluator to each member [of a policy-making group], encouraging the group to give high priority to airing objections and doubts.
>
> [The] setting up [of] several independent policy-planning and evaluation groups to work on the same policy question, each carrying out its deliberations under a different leader.
>
> One or more outside experts or qualified colleagues . . . who are not core members of the policy-making group should be invited to each meeting on a staggered basis and should be encouraged to challenge the views of the core members.

At least one member should be assigned the role of devil's advocate.[26]

Janis recognizes the risks and difficulties in implementing his proposals, yet the steps outlined aboved would clearly be helpful in encouraging constructive dissent and lessening cult-like behavior at the highest levels of government. We can be confident that these procedures are practical because they have been used successfully already.

Following the Bay of Pigs disaster, President Kennedy sought to understand why his administration had blundered so badly, and when the next crisis occurred he put a much different system into operation.

In October of 1962, the discovery that the Soviet Union was installing nuclear missiles in Cuba spurred Kennedy to convene a group of high-level advisors to decide how to deal with the threat. Five of the key men selected had participated in the Bay of Pigs planning group: Rusk, McNamara, Dillon, Bundy and Robert Kennedy. As before, they met under great time pressure, for they believed it was essential to take action before the missile sites became operational.

Rightly or wrongly, Kennedy ruled out a diplomatic approach. He made it clear that the situation was unacceptable and that the group task was to decide on the best form of coercive action to force the removal of the missiles from Cuba.

This time, the team did not try to satisfy an impatient president by obtaining a quick consensus. They reacted quite differently, not only because they remembered what had happened at the Bay of Pigs, but because Kennedy saw to it that their deliberations took place under quite different procedures.

Each participant was expected to function as an independent critical thinker, addressing the problem in its entirety and not primarily as a spokesperson for the agency they represented. Robert Kennedy and Theodore Sorensen were given special roles to guard the group against superficial analysis. No formal agenda was imposed; discussions were free and far-ranging. Outside experts were invited to give opinions and then were questioned closely. If visitors to the group remained silent, they were specifically asked to state their observations and comments. Sub-groups were formed to work independently on the same problem and then meet to compare findings. From time to time, President Kennedy absented himself from the group, especially in early phases when many different alternatives were first considered.[27]

As an example of the results of this different process, Robert Kennedy, who during the Bay of Pigs discussion had chided dissenters, this time guarded against premature closure of options. When an airstrike was proposed as the only option, he advised reconsideration. "'Surely,' he asserted, 'there was some course in between bombing and doing nothing.' . . . By the end of the first day of meetings the committee had seriously discussed at least ten alternatives."[28]

There was no false confidence, no shoving aside of the frightful risks that attended each option. The participants were encouraged to challenge each other's assumptions, to speak their minds frankly and treat each other, as well as outside visitors and consultants, as equals. Dissent was recognized as vital to finding a way to the most realistic action.

This process was often stressful for committee members, leading to unpleasant arguments, agitation, and sleepless nights. The discussions went on for days and seemed interminable, but in the end the blockade plan was decided upon. Furthermore, contingency plans were worked out in full detail to cope with a variety of possible Soviet responses. Nothing was taken for granted.

> As a result of the thorough review of *all the drawbacks* [emphasis added], the recommendations the group gave to the President included much more than strategic military guidelines. The group worked out in considerable detail ways of handling a variety of political, legal, and diplomatic ramifications, which, if neglected, could cause a blockade attempt to fail.[29]

The contrast to the Bay of Pigs deliberations is striking. Even if the blockade had not worked, the chances of success had been maximized and contingency responses were thought through and put in place. The practice of welcoming dissent—uncomfortable and disconcerting as it can be—proved immensely practical.

Unfortunately, it seems that presidents do not always learn from their predecessors. After the Tower report on the Iran-contra affair was released, Senator Nancy Kassenbaum, a Republican member of the Senate Foreign Relations Committee, commented,

The underlying problem in all this is a lack of respect for dissent. The president has not been able to hear all sides of an issue. And we saw the same thing on SDI, contra aid, South Africa, and, of course, the budget. People in the administration who challenge policy are just shunted aside. That's the basic flaw in the process.[30]

The Eye-Level World

Probably the most common everyday cult behavior is devaluation of the outsider. As discussed earlier, we do this not only to feel superior, but also as a defense against recognizing those things in ourselves about which we feel ashamed and inferior; human beings tend to see someone else as embodying the defects they themselves deny. This projection of badness interferes with a realistic assessment of another's intentions. Frequently, it serves to justify violence. In contrast, an eye-level view recognizes defects and hurtful actions in the other without adopting a superior position or lowering the other to subhuman status.

In the service of realism, it is important to diminish projection and establish an eye-level perspective, for in our fears, hopes, and capacity for nobility as well as self-deception, we can recognize each other, see that "the enemy is us." Measures that reveal our similarities to the outsider, not just our differences, are very helpful. The reader may object that such perceptions of the hostile outsider must be mutual, that if we perceive the humanness and similarity of our enemies while they do not so perceive us, then we are at a fatal disadvantage. This is simply not so. Perceiving the other person without the distortion imposed by projection permits us to see more clearly, to respond more realistically. That response might be either aggressive or conciliatory, depending upon what is called for by the reality of the situation (not by the product of projective defenses). Such realism is always an advantage, especially in our dealings with other nations, other people— "the foreigner." At such times, cult behavior is likely to be most intense and mutual recognition most memorable.

Forty years after the Allied landing in France, an American soldier recalled that time:

Arruda nodded, his hands touching the green napkin with its rough map of a 40-year-old battlefield. "I'd like to go back to the places I landed, the places I fought," he said, "to see the city of Cherbourg . . ."

And maybe he could find the spot in a field outside St. Lo where he stood up at the same time as a German officer who was only a few feet away.

"We looked at each other for the longest time, just staring," said Arruda. "I knew he had his troops behind him and he knew my people were back there. I was thinking, 'Hey, this son of a bitch is just like me.' And we both of us turned around very slowly and walked away from each other." [31]

How can this eye-level perception be fostered? As we know from experience, actual contact helps greatly—if the contact occurs with enough informality for the participants' humanity to emerge. At the international level, citizen exchanges between countries, involvement in joint work projects, and shared living are all moves in the right direction. Unfortunately, the people who participate in such activities usually do not occupy positions in the higher echelons of government, although those leaders need that experience more than anyone else. High-level contact—frequently and for days at a time—is one thing that might cost little but could significantly reduce projection. (Such extended personal meetings resulted in Ronald Reagan's stroll in Red Square with his arm around the shoulders of Mikhail Gorbachev, the "evil empire" relegated to "another time, another era.")

In many situations eye-level perception can be enhanced by using encounter group techniques developed in the sixties and early seventies to increase the depth of communication among group members. Carl Rogers used these techniques successfully to promote understanding between antagonistic national groups.[32] I believe they could be utilized to make perception more realistic between opposing factions at all levels. Increasing the range of tools with which national and international problems might be resolved would certainly be desirable.

．　■　■

Mahatma Gandhi was successful in achieving political change through non-violent civil disobedience. He served as a model for Kaunda in Zambia, Martin Luther King in Montgomery, Alabama, and many others. Gandhi's principles of action were the opposite of cult behavior. He stressed putting oneself in the place of the opponent, respecting his or her potential goodness, and recognizing that you may be in error. Gandhi was quite explicit about what was required.

> I want you to feel like loving your opponents, and the way to do it is to give them same credit for honesty of purpose which you would claim for yourself.
> . . . . It is true that they have their ends to serve. But so have we our ends to serve. Only we consider our ends to be pure and, therefore, selfless. But who are we to determine where selflessness ends and selfishness begins?
> . . . . Immediately we begin to think of things as our opponents think of them we shall be able to do them full justice.
> . . . . Three-fourths of the miseries and misunderstandings in the world will disappear, if we step into the shoes of our adversaries and understand their standpoint.[33]

These principles directly combat devaluation and aim at establishing eye-level relationships that eliminate all self-righteousness. Gandhi went further and stressed that humiliation of the opponent was not permissible; great care was to be taken to maintain the opponent's dignity and self-respect. At every step Gandhi was concerned that the opponent save face, and this concern was a tribute to his realism. General Smuts remarked after experiencing Gandhi in South Africa. "It was my fate to be the antagonist of a man for whom even then I had the highest respect . . . He never forgot the human background of the situation."[34]

Unfortunately, the vast majority of Gandhi's followers venerated him as a saint, to the detriment of the eye-level relationship he advocated in dealing with adversaries. They responded to him as to a parent ("Bapu"), with the dependency dynamics outlined for cults. As Erik Erikson's study made clear, Gandhi was quite capable of being authoritarian, tyrannical, and unjust to his own immediate family and disciples.[35] Everyone, even one called saint or genius, is flawed. The failure of Gandhi—like the failure of every great mass leader in human history—was not in having flaws, but in not freeing his followers from cult behavior. The awful violence between Moslems and Hindus that took place during his lifetime and afterwards was a typical product of cult psychology. In the name of religions that advocate justice, mercy, generosity, and humility, the most barbarous atrocities were committed by each group against the other. Gandhi could stop them by fasting, but when Gandhi was gone most showed they had learned nothing.

.   .   .

Characteristically, cults subordinate ethical and moral standards to the particular aims of the group and leader. These are called higher purposes, usually put in terms of saving the world (as when the needs of Clara's child were made secondary to the needs of Life Force). In political situations in America, "saving the world for democracy," "overthrowing communism," "fighting terrorism," or the "war on drugs" are cited to justify illegal and immoral actions by the government. Undoubtedly, situations arise in which hard choices must be made; but often government officials use "higher purposes" to justify unsavory operations that are remarkably ineffective, if not disastrous: the internment of the Japanese in 1942, the Bay of Pigs, the Tonkin Gulf incident, the bombing of Cambodia, the overthrow of Allende and the sale of arms to Iran, among many others. Cult thinking is seldom realistic.

In contrast, the deliberations of the Cuban missile crisis planning group were guided by a basic approach strikingly consistent with Gandhi's, one which included concern for the ethics of any proposed action, putting onself in the opponent's place, and being careful to avoid humiliating him. The first days of the missile crisis group's discussions were occupied with the morality of an air strike against the Cuban bases. This proposal advanced by the military was at first favored by President Kennedy and Douglas Dillon. However, George Ball vigorously objected that such a surprise attack would be counter to our own traditions and harm our moral standing. Robert Kennedy agreed, pointing out the loss of innocent lives that would result and that such an action would be a "Pearl Harbor in reverse," going against our humanitarian ideals. Robert McNamara also agreed and in his retrospective account makes it clear that Robert Kennedy's stress on moral values was an important influence which resulted in the abandonment of the air strike option in favor of a blockade:

His [Robert Kennedy's] contribution was far more than administrative . . . he opposed a massive surprise attack of a large country on a small country because he believed such an attack to be inhuman, contrary to our traditions and ideals and an act of brutality for which the world would never forgive us.[36]

In practice, *realpolitik* (which ignores ethical considerations) usually is cult-like in that it is linked to a devaluation of the enemy, to stereotyping and self-righteousness. In contrast, realism requires putting oneself in one's opponent's place if one is to understand and predict the opponent's actions. In typical Gandhi fashion, the Cuban Missile Group did just that.

Most members viewed their opposite numbers in the Kremlin as no less rational than themselves. . . . Often the members of the group set themselves the task of trying to predict how the enemy would react to one or another course of action by deliberately trying to imagine themselves in the Soviet leaders' place. . . . Without denying the cunning and deceit of the Soviet leaders, the group adopted the working assumption that the Soviet Union would not be likely to initiate a war unless unduly provoked. . . . Rusk and other members . . . urged the group to choose a response that the Soviet leaders could clearly see offered them a way out. . . . An important argument that led the group to regard a naval blockade as much more prudent than any alternative military response was precisely that this low-level action could serve as an unmistakable indication of America's strong intention to eliminate the missile bases without confronting the Soviet leaders with a belligerent act that would be "sudden or humiliating."[37]

Avoiding situations that would embarrass the Soviets was an important strategic consideration. Consequently, the first ship boarded was not Soviet, but a Lebanese freighter under charter to the Soviets. At every step, including American replies to Soviet proposals, care was taken to avoid provocative, unduly threatening, or humiliating actions.

Robert Kennedy concluded, "A final lesson of the Cuban missile crisis is the importance of placing ourselves in the other country's shoes."[38]

Gandhi would agree.

■ ■ ■

Two primary cult behaviors, compliance with the group and dependence on a leader, have served necessary functions in the survival of the human race. They are very important in childhood, where they provide safety, security, encouragement, and support. Groups and leaders have legitimate functions for adults as well. They can stimulate, reinforce, and guide individuals' energies in constructive ways; they provide meaning and counter isolation and loneliness with acceptance and warmth. But the fantasy of parents must be transcended by adults; for us it is no longer function. Indeed, regressive dependency makes our survival and progress more difficult because reality must be distorted in order to construct shepherds out of sheep.

Adult human beings stand together in a horizontal plane, but they all too often try to organize it vertically. The reader may assume that the eye-level world is his or her basic perspective. It hasn't been for me. Whenever I gave a public lecture I noticed that immediately afterward I felt let-down, disappointed, no matter how well the audience had responded. Eventually, I realized that I was preparing my lectures as if the authority figures of my early professional years would be listening. At the periphery of my mind was an image of them seated in the back of the auditorium. There were no specific faces, just a row of sceptical shadows. I worked hard shaping and rehearsing my lectures to convince them of the rightness of my views, to win their approval, their grudging admiration. But when I stepped up on the platform and looked over the audience I could see that they weren't there. They hadn't come.

This fantasy of fathers, this vertical perspective, had been hidden from me until my disappointment alerted me to it. I know I am not alone in this. I can recognize the persistence of what I call the parent-world in the attitude and behavior of my friends, in the implicit views of authors whose books I read, and in the statements of public figures. As a psychotherapist, I find the parent-world in the fantasies of people with normal and useful adult positions—teachers, housewives, carpenters, lawyers, executives, students—people in all the occupations that comprise everyday society. The evidence is strong that all of us show the effects of having been raised in a hierarchical world in which there were those above us and those below. From such a perspective there is always a higher authority.

Perhaps I can bring this home with another demonstration. Morality is usually experienced as a given, as a code whose violation brings punishment or, at the least, guilt. Most people, if they look within, discover a subtle fantasy that someone or something is keeping score of their good and bad deeds and that in the future—usually after death—there will be a settling-up. If you doubt this, try an experiment. Imagine that there will be no ultimate retribution for anything you do, no denial of Heaven to the wicked. Imagine that whether you behave like a saint or a sadist, are kind or cruel, generous or selfish, it will make no difference when you die. How you behave is entirely up to you. Do whatever you want, there are no celestial consequences. Imagining this, what would you do, how would you behave? (Try it now. Take a few minutes to see what it is like.)

The first time I did this experiment it was an uneasy experience. Imagining myself to be the only authority gave me a sensation of wobby morality. Principles that had seemed rock solid were swaying in the breeze, and in that moment I did not know how I would choose to act if there were no retribution, no reward, no eventual Judgment Day. That uncertainty brought into focus the assumptions and dynamics of my ordinary world and made me realize how my eyes too frequently gaze back over my shoulder at the invisible, hovering parents of adult childhood. When I asked friends to imagine the same parentless scenario I could see it was unfamiliar to them also, even startling and uncomfortable, although they were independent and self-supporting—adult by all usual criteria.

■   ■   ■

If gods do not occupy the heavens, and wise parents do not head governments, if there are no experts without error and prejudice, how can we find our way to a home that is not a dream? The child's home is in the past. We may try to create a home again in the families in which we are the parent. Wife, husband, and children can provide a place where love is given and received. But as adults it is not the same because our reality is different. We are far from being the parent we imagined as a child; pretending doesn't work. Can there be home for us?

The eye-level world is the perspective that arises when the parents in the sky disappear and their images superimposed on other people dissolve and vanish. As you look around, no one towers above you, everyone looks back at the same human height. Although the parents are gone, the landscape is not threatening, it spreads out in all directions, inviting exploration. It is open and calm, in contrast to the world of childhood fears.

The child fears that the disappearance of parents would release anarchy, hatred, and destruction because in the parents' world the child knows no power, no control that is not imposed. In the eye-level world freedom is of a different kind, more responsible than before because the choices are your own, they are uncoerced and unbribed. "Free will is the experience of being tthe author of the law you obey." This world is different from that shaped by the dependency dream.

Although we have no parents in the eye-level world, when we face each other we find companions. We share the same need for meaning, the same intimations of transcendence, the certainty of death, the saving joy of love. We can sense a new connection, a linking of equals that makes all of us one family, yet individuals. Only in the eye-level world do we emerge as ourselves, true to our own perceptions and strengths, able to respond realistically to the world that surrounds us.

Cult behavior is the expression of the dependency dream. It is a self-deception more serious than may at first appear, for at this point in history problems confront us that threaten everyone on earth: nuclear weapons, contamination of the environment, spiraling populations. To solve these problems we need as much realism as possible, and realism is the first casualty of cult behavior. We must leave the security of the cult circle and move forward into the eye-level world. Whether we are inclined to lead or to follow, let us hope we can see that cult behavior is too risky, the comfort of its fantasy a lie. Reality may be more uncertain than we wish but its freedom is a bountiful reward. When the gods and demons disappear a different world appears, rich in sunlight and storm but without fear. Standing together on that level plain, we find ourselves in a new home, one that is quite real. There are no outsiders. And it is worth more than any dream.

Notes

Introduction

1. Robert Lifton, *Thought Reform and the Psychology of Totalism* (New York: W. W. Norton, 1969).

Chapter 1: The Cult Mirror

1. Seminar sponsored by the Center for the Study of New Religious Movements, in Berkeley, California, 1980–81.

Chapter 3: Compliance with the Group

1. For a convincing analysis of this in French society see Pierre Bourdieu, *Distinction: A Social Critique of the Judgment of Taste* (Cambridge, Mass.: Harvard University Press, 1984).

2. The analyst is quoted in Janet Malcolm, *Psychoanalysis: The Impossible Profession* (New York: Alfred Knopf, 1981), p. 53.

3. Robert B. Cialdini, *Influence—Science and Practice* (Glenview, Illinois: Scott, Foresman and Company, 1985), pp. 101–2.

4. Ibid., p. 98.

5. Sigmund Freud, "Group Psychology and the Analysis of the Ego," in *The Standard Edition of the Complete Psychological Works of Sigmund Freud*, ed. J. Strachey (London: The Hogarth Press, 1955), vol. 18, p. 76.

6. Ibid., pp. 122, 123.

7. Ibid., pp. 124, 125.

8. Margaret Rioch, "The Work of Wilfred Bion on Groups" in Arthur D. Colman and W. Harold Bexton, *Group Relations Reader* (Sausalito, California: GREX, 1975), p. 24.

9. A. Colman, "Group Consciousness as a Developmental Phase," Ibid., pp. 35–42.

10. Rosabeth Kanter, *Commitment and Community: Communes and Utopias in Sociological Perspective* (Cambridge, Mass.: Harvard University Press, 1972), p. 87.

11. Ibid., p. 88.

12. Alfons Heck, *A Child of Hitler: Germany in the Days When God Wore a Swastika* (Frederick, Colorado: Renaissance House, 1985).

13. Lowell Streiker, *The Gospel Time Bomb: Ultrafundamentalism and the Future of America* (Buffalo, New York: Prometheus Books, 1984), p. 81.

14. Ibid., p. 81.

15. See Walter Hilton, *The Scale of Perfection* (London: Burns & Oates, 1953), pp. 14, 15; St. John of the Cross, *The Complete Works of St. John of the Cross* (Westminster: Newman Press, 1953) vol. 1, p. 457; and Philip Kapleau, *The Three Pillars of Zen* (Boston: Beacon Press, 1967), p. 40.

16. Diane Margolis, *The Managers: Corporate Life in America* (New York: Murrow, 1979), pp. 107–09.

17. Quoted in Ibid., p. 52.

18. Quoted in Ken Auletta, *The Art of Corporate Success: The Story of Schlumberger* (New York: Viking Penguin, 1984), pp. 131, 132.

19. Rosabeth Kanter, *Men and Women of the Corporation* (New York: Basic Books, 1977), p. 110.

20. Quoted in Richard Pascale and Anthony Athos, *The Art of Japanese Management: Applications for American Executives* (New York: Warner Books, 1981), p. 115.

21. Margolis, pp. 107, 109.

22. Richard Pascale, "The Paradox of 'Corporate Culture': Reconciling Ourselves to Socialization" (Research Paper No. 738, Stanford University 1984, Graduate School of Business), p. 5.

23. Pascale and Athos, p. 286.

24. Pascale, p. 6–7.

25. Quoted in Barbara Underwood and Betty Underwood, *Hostage to Heaven* (New York: Clarkson Potter, 1979), p. 70.

26. Margolis, pp. 62–63.

27. Auletta, p. 161.

28. Quoted in Ibid., pp. 123–124.

29. Terrance Deal and Allen Kennedy, *Corporate Cultures: The Rights and Rituals of Corporate Life* (Reading, Mass.: Addison-Wesley 1982) p. 195.

30. Thomas Peters and Robert Waterman, Jr., *In Search of Excellence: Lessons from America's Best-Run Companies* (New York: Warner Books, 1982), p. 78.

31. Pascale and Athos, p. 320.

32. Paul Brodeur, "The Asbestos Industry on Trial," *The New Yorker*, 10, 17, and 24 June 1985.

33. Morton Mintz, *At Any Cost: Corporate Greed, Women and the Dalkon Shield* (New York: Pantheon, 1986).

34. Margaret Rioch, "'All We Like Sheep—': Followers and Leaders," in Colman and Bexton, p. 170.

Chapter 4: Dependence on a Leader

1. Craig Karpel, "The Gnomes of Bilderberg," *Penthouse*, May 1981, p. 152.

2. Ibid.

3. James Barber, *The New York Times*, 26 April 1984, p. 25.

4. Rioch, "'All We Like Sheep—,'" p. 159.

5. Investigative Poetry Group, *The Party: A Chronological Perspective on a Confrontation at a Buddhist Seminary* (Woodstock, New York: Poetry, Crime and Culture Press, 1977), p. 55.

6. Ibid., p. 56.

7. Quoted in Gary Wills, *Reagan's America*, (New York: Penguin Books, 1988), p. 355.

8. Peters and Waterman, p.84.

9. Harold Geneen (with A. Moscow), *Managing*, (Garden City, New York: Doubleday, 1984), p. 144.

10. Quoted in J. Patrick Wright, *On A Clear Day You Can See Forever* (New York: Avon, 1979), p. 68.

11. Peters and Waterman, pp. 31, 46, 48.

12. Erich Fromm, *Escape From Freedom* (New York: Farrar & Rinehart, 1941).

13. Peters and Waterman, p. 68.

14. Cornelle Maier, interview with the author, 11 June 1986.

15. Christopher Byron, *The Fanciest Dive* (New York: Norton, 1986), p. 103.

16. Quoted in Margolis, p. 93.

17. St. John of the Cross, vol. 1, p. 457.

18. Quoted in Flo Conway and Jim Siegelman, *Holy Terror: The Fundamentalist War on America's Freedoms in Religion, Politics, and Our Private Lives* (New York: Dell, 1982), p. 283.

19. R. Knight, "Determinism, 'Freedom,' and Psychotherapy," *Psychiatry*, 9 (1946), pp. 251–62.

20. Idries Shah, *The Dermis Probe* (London: Octagon Press, 1980), p. 158.

21. Joan Chittister, "No Time for Tying Cats," in *Midwives of the Future*, ed. Ann Ware (Kansas City, Missouri: Leaven Press, 1985), p. 7.

22. Quoted in Conway and Siegelman, p. 234.

23. James Kavanaugh, *A Modern Priest Looks At His Outdated Church* (New York: Trident Press, 1967), p. 178.

24. Liz Harris, "Holy Days," *The New Yorker*, 30 September 1985, p. 92.

25. Barbara Underwood and Betty Underwood, *Hostage to Heaven* (New York: Clarkson Potter, 1979).

26. Quoted in Conway and Siegelman, p. 252.

27. Arthur J. Deikman, "Comments on the GAP Report on Mysticism," *Journal of Nervous and Mental Disease*, 165:3 (1977), pp. 213–217.

28. Arthur J. Deikman, *The Observing Self: Mysticism and Psychotherapy* (Boston: Beacon Press, 1982).

29. Arthur J. Deikman, "The Evaluation of Spiritual and Utopian Groups," *Journal of Humanistic Psychology*, 23:3 (1983), pp. 8–19.

30. Idries Shah, *The Way of the Sufi* (London: Jonathan Cape, 1968), p. 219.

31. Quoted in Ann Ware, ed., *Midwives of the Future* (Kansas City, Missouri: Leaven Press, 1985), p. 237.

32. M. K. Temerlin and J. W. Temerlin, "Psychotherapy Cults: An Iatrogenic Perversion," *Psychotherapy: Theory, Research and Practice*, 19:2 (1982), pp. 131–41.

33. Otto F. Kernberg, "Institutional Problems of Psychoanalytic Education," *Journal of the American Psychiatric Association*, 34 (1986), pp. 799–834.

34. Ibid.

35. Jacob A. Arlow, "Some Dilemmas in Psychoanalytic Education," *Journal of the American Psychiatric Association* 20 (1972), pp. 556–566.

36. Ibid.

37. Arthur Schlesinger, *A Thousand Days* (Boston: Fawcett/Houghton Mifflin, 1965) p. 259.

38. Irving Janis, *Victims of Groupthink* (Boston: Houghton Mifflin, 1972).

39. Stanley Milgram, *Obedience to Authority: An Experimental View* (San Francisco: Harper and Row, 1974).

40. Ibid., pp. 8–9.

41. Noam Chomsky quoted in William Barrett et al., "Human Rights and American Foreign Policy: A Symposium," *Commentary* 72 (November 1981), pp. 30–31.

Chapter 5: Devaluing the Outsider

1. Jack Katz, *Seductions of Crime: Moral and Sensual Attractions in Doing Evil* (New York: Basic Books, 1988), pp. 36, 37.

2. Quoted in Al Santoli, *Everything We Had* (New York: Random House, 1981), p. 70.

3. *The American Psychiatric Association's Psychiatric Glossary*, ed. A. Werner et al. (Washington, D.C.: American Psychiatric Press, 1984), p. 110.

4. Hannah Arendt, *Eichmann in Jerusalem* (New York: Viking, 1963).

5. Stanley Milgram, *Obedience to Authority* (New York: Harper and Row, 1974).

6. Philip Zimbardo, et al., "The Psychology of Imprisonment: Privation, Power and Pathology," in *Doing Unto Others: Explorations in Social Behavior*, ed. Z. Rubin (Englewood Cliffs, New Jersey: Prentice-Hall, 1974).

7. Quoted in Frances Fitzgerald, "A Reporter At Large: A Disciplined, Charging Army," *The New Yorker*, 18 May 1981, p. 107.

8. Quoted in *Harper's*, April 1985, p. 17.

9. Quoted in *Harper's*, December 1983, p. 55.

10. Martin Marty, *A Nation of Believers* (Chicago: University of Chicago Press, 1976), pp. 81, 82.

11. For further discussion, see Arthur J. Deikman and Lee C. Whitaker, "Humanizing a Psychiatric Ward: Changing from Drugs to Psychotherapy," *Psychotherapy: Theory, Research and Practice* 17, pp. 85–93.

12. Todd Gitlin, *The Whole World Is Watching: Mass Media in the Making and Unmaking of the New Left* (Berkeley: University of California Press, 1980), p. 48 (note 22).

13. Ibid., p. 4.

14. Daniel Hallin, *The Uncensored War: The Media and Vietnam* (New York: Oxford University Press, 1982), p. 200.

15. Stephen Cohen, *Sovieticus: American Perceptions and Soviet Realities* (New York: W. W. Norton, 1985), pp. 29, 30.

16. Herbert York, *The Advisers: Oppenheimer, Teller and the Superbomb* (San Francisco: W. H. Freeman, 1976), p. 34.

17. Philip Knightley, *The Second Oldest Profession: Spies and Spying in the Twentieth Century* (New York: W. W. Norton, 1986), pp. 264–265.

18. Robert Jervis, *Perception and Misperception in International Politics* (Princeton: Princeton University Press, 1976), p. 65.

19. Ibid., p. 61.

20. Ibid., p. 68.

21. Ibid., p. 61.

22. Arnold Kanter, *Defense Politics: A Budgetary Perspective* (Chicago: University of Chicago Press, 1975).

23. Peter H. Wyden, *Bay of Pigs: The Untold Story* (New York: Simon & Schuster, 1979), p. 8.

24. Quoted in Walter Capps, *The Unfinished War: Vietnam and the American Conscience*, 2d ed. (Boston: Beacon Press, 1990), pp. 92–93.

25. Ronald Reagan, Speech to the 41st Annual Convention of the National Association of Evangelicals, Orlando, Florida, 8 March 1983.

26. Ibid.

27. Jervis, p. 323.

28. Ibid., p. 328.

29. Randy Shilts, *And The Band Played On: People Politics and the Aids Epidemic* (New York: St. Martin's Press, 1987).

30. Ibid., p. 335.

Chapter 6: Avoiding Dissent

1. Marc Galanter, "Psychological Induction Into the Large-Group: Findings from a Modern Religious Sect," *American Journal of Psychiatry* 137 (1980), pp. 1574–1579.

2. Ben Bagdikian, *The Media Monopoly,* 2d ed. (Boston: Beacon Press, 1987), pp. ix, x.

3. Ben Bagdikian, *The Media Monopoly* (Boston: Beacon Press, 1983).

4. Ibid., p. 24.

5. "NBC Snips Out Reference to GE," *San Francisco Chronicle,* 4 December 1989.

6. Bagdikian, 1987, pp. 27–39.

7. U.S. Bureau of Labor Statistics, cited in "Harper's Index," *Harper's Magazine,* August 1987, p. 11.

8. *Extra* 2:2, Sept/Oct 1988.

9. Bagdikian, 1987, p. 123.

10. George Gerbner et al., "Charting the Mainstream" in Doris Graber, ed. *Media Power in Politics* (Washington, D.C.: CQ Press, 1984), pp. 119–20.

11. Ibid., p. 129.

12. Bagdikian, 1987, p. 157.

13. Ibid., pp. 156–157.

14. Quoted in Ibid., pp. 171–172.

15. Ibid., p. 167.

16. *San Francisco Chronicle,* 22 October 1986.

17. Bagdikian, 1987, p. 155.

18. Bernard Roshco, *Newsmaking* (Chicago: University of Chicago Press, 1975), p. 115.

19. Warren Weaver, *Both Your Houses* (New York: Praeger Publishers, 1972), p. 12.

20. Mark Hertsgaard, *On Bended Knee: The Press and the Reagan Presidency* (New York: Schocken Books, 1988), p. 347.

21. *Extra* 2:4, Jan/Feb 1989.

22. Quoted in Robert Stein, *Media Power: Who Is Shaping Your Picture of the World?* (Boston: Houghton Mifflin, 1972), p. 30.

23. Hallin, p. 50.

24. Ibid., p. 208.

25. David Altheide, "Iran vs. U.S. TV News: The Hostage Story out of Context," in Doris Graber (ed.), *Media Power in Politics*, p. 300.

26. Hallin, p. 99.

27. E. Herman, N. Chomsky, *Manufacturing Consent—The Political Economy of the Mass Media* (New York: Pantheon, 1988), p. 348.

28. Herbert Gans, *Deciding What's News—A Study of CBS Evening News, NBC Nightly News, Newsweek, and Time* (New York: Pantheon, 1979), p. 277.

29. Bagdikian, 1987, p. 218.

30. Quoted in Wright, pp. 42, 47.

31. Ibid., pp. 65, 66.

32. Byron, p. 105.

33. Ibid., p. 201.

34. Henry Cooper, Jr., "Letter From The Space Center," *The New Yorker*, 10 November 1986.

35. Wyden, pp. 148, 149.

36. Walter Reich, "Psychiatry's Second Coming," *Psychiatry*, vol. 45 (August 1982).

37. See Loren R. Mosher's review of *Recovery from Schizophrenia: Psychiatry and Political Economy*, by Richard Warner, in *American Journal of Psychiatry* 144:7, July 1987, p. 956.

38. J. Sanbourne Bockhoven and Harry C. Solomon, "Comparison of Two Five-Year Follow-Up Studies: 1947 to 1952 and 1967 to 1972," *American Journal of Psychiatry* 132:8, August 1975, pp. 796–801.

39. J. Sanbourne Bockhoven, *Moral Treatment in American Psychiatry* (New York: Springer Publishing Company, 1963).

40. John M. Kane, "Treatment of Schizophrenia," *Schizophrenia Bulletin* 13:1, 1987, pp. 133–156.

41. Alfred H. Stanton and Morris S. Schwartz, *The Mental Hospital: A Study of Institutional Participation in Psychiatric Illness and Treatment* (New York: Basic Books, 1954), p. 345.

42. Ibid., p. 408.

43. *San Francisco Chronicle*, 20 August 1986.

44. Ibid.

45. Flo Conway and Alan Siegelman, p. 86.

46. Lowell Streiker, p. 91.

47. Conway and Siegelman, p. 144.

48. Elizabeth Bugental, private communication to the author.

49. M. Wong, *Nun: A Memoir* (New York: Harcourt Brace Jovanovich, 1983), p. 300.

50. Liz Harris, "Holy Days," *The New Yorker,* 30 September 1985, p. 88.

51. Deikman, "The Evaluation of Spiritual and Utopian Groups."

52. Tom Wicker, *On Press—A Top Reporter's Life in, and Reflections on, American Journalism* (New York: Viking, 1978), p. 195.

Chapter 7: Exit from the Cult

1. Quoted in Robert McNamara, "The Military Role of Nuclear Weapons," *Foreign Affairs,* Fall 1983.

2. Hyman Rickover, in testimony during congressional hearings of the Joint Economic Committee, reported in *Rolling Stone,* 1 April 1982.

3. Quoted in *San Francisco Chronicle,* 9 May 1982.

4. William Morris, ed., *The American Heritage Dictionary,* p. 474.

5. Barbara Tuchman, *The March of Folly* (New York: Alfred A. Knopf, 1984), p. 7.

6. Ibid., p. 32.

7. Maya Pines, "Unlearning Blind Obedience in German Schools," *Psychology Today,* 15:5, May 1981, p. 65.

8. Ibid.

9. Idries Shah, *Observations,* comp. Lindsi Tarabdar and Zoltan Na'lbandev (London: Designist Communications, 1982), p. 27.

10. Wright, p. 223.

11. Pascale and Athos, p. 52.

12. Ibid., p. 59.

13. Auletta, pp. 90, 95.

14. Wright.

15. Jacques Ellul, *Propaganda: The Formation of Men's Attitudes* (New York: Knopf, 1965).

16. Ibid.

17. Quoted in B. Berelson, P. Lazarfeld and W. McPhee, *Voting: A Study of Opinion Formation in a Presidential Campaign* (Chicago: University of Chicago Press, 1954), pp. 314, 315.

18. Ibid.

19. Geneen, pp. 133, 134.

20. Pascale and Athos, p. 97.

21. Ibid., p. 110.

22. Ibid., pp. 269, 270.

23. Lee Iococca (with William Novak), *Iococca: An Autobiography* (New York: Bantam Books, 1984).

24. Byron, op. cit.

25. William Manchester, *American Caesar: Douglas MacArthur 1880–1964* (Boston: Little, Brown and Co., 1978), p. 215.

26. Janis, pp. 209–215.

27. Ibid., pp. 138–149.

28. Ibid., p. 150.

29. Ibid., p. 152.

30. Quoted in George Lardner, Jr., "The Tower Report Sows a Mine Field for the Administration," *The Washington Post National Weekly Edition* 9 March 1987, p. 13.

31. "D-Day veterans remember their baptism by fire," *San Francisco Sunday Examiner and Chronicle,* 3 June 1984.

32. Carl Rogers, "The Rust Workshop: A Personal Overview," *Journal of Humanistic Psychology* 26:3, Summer 1986, pp. 23–45.

33. Mohandas Gandhi, *Non-Violent Resistance (Satyagraha)* (New York: Schocken Books, 1961), p. 193.

34. Louis Fischer, *The Life of Gandhi* (New York: Harper & Brothers, 1950), p. 117.

35. Erik Erikson, *Gandhi's Truth* (New York: W. W. Norton, 1969).

36. Robert McNamara, Introduction to Robert Kennedy's *Thirteen Days* (New York: W. W. Norton, 1969), pp. 14, 15.

37. Janis, pp. 159, 160.

38. Janis, p. 164.

Index